EMERGENCY ROOM
DIARY

BY THE SAME AUTHOR

EMERGENCY ROOM DIARY

Theodore Isaac Rubin M.D.

GROSSET & DUNLAP
A National General Company
Publishers   New York

Copyright © 1972 by Theodore Isaac Rubin
All rights reserved
Published simultaneously in Canada

Library of Congress catalog card number: 72–79619
ISBN 0–448–01555–2

Printed in the United States of America

To my son, Jeff, who is
currently interning at the Metropolitan Hospital Center
in New York City and is paid $12,000 a year.
As an intern I was paid $75 a month—
so the Rubins have made considerable progress.

PREFACE

I worked in the Emergency Room about twenty years ago in the last four months of a year's rotating internship. I started to work in the E.R. full time—we all wandered in and out of it even when we were on other services—after I had already completed medicine, obstetrics, and surgery. Rereading my diary of that time makes me feel a bit embarrassed by the somewhat unsophisticated young man who lived it—but I feel rather satisfied with him too. Those four months and the following year of weekends in the E.R. made a deep and lasting impression. I feel that my E.R. time, more than anything else during that period of my life, contributed to personal growth, a sense of professional responsibility, and the ability to make decisions. This all sounds rather ponderous, but it is nevertheless true. The E.R. did a fast and remarkably thorough job, in the short time I spent there, of ridding me of many childish illusions regarding the human condition, more specifically those involving medicine, doctors, and myself. It also helped prepare me for future confrontations. There have been many things that have fazed me since those days, but I've not been nearly as shook up or vulnerable as I might have been without the E.R. experience. In short, it was invaluable in helping me to grow up, humanly and professionally—and of course there is no dichotomy there. Both are part of the same process. I also feel that an important facet of my development as a psychiatrist and therapist has its roots in this E.R. experience of mine.

Comparing notes with Jeff, little has changed in the last twenty years. There are some new lab tests and medical advances but little of this affects E.R. patients or their treatment. Interns work fewer hours and there are not as many nights on duty, but responsibility for people in every conceivable kind of medical difficulty is the same now as it was then.

The facts are true. All of it has happened. I have not named the place and I've changed the names of the people for obvious reasons.

The Introduction that follows describes the emergency room in general terms—its purpose, staff, equipment, procedures—to establish for the reader the world in which I worked for those four months. A glossary of specific medical terms and hospital jargon is given at the end of the book.

INTRODUCTION

The hospital was considered moderate size, a 250-bed, non-profit, community hospital in southern California. The place had the usual surgical, medical, gynecological, and pediatric services, plus appropriate clinics.

The emergency department, and it was a department, was unusual. It was larger, better equipped, and more efficiently run than E.R.s of much larger hospitals. Indeed, it contributed considerably to the public prestige of the hospital and may well have been one of its most important departments. This was largely due to the fact that the hospital covered most of West Los Angeles, a most prolific area for all kinds of medical emergencies. Its areas of responsibility included a large number of industrial sites, huge beach areas, large residential areas of nearly all economic levels, and the various Los Angeles canyons as well as the coast highway. The last alone was murderous enough to keep an ordinary E.R. going full time.

Ideally, the emergency room functions solely for the treatment of surgical and medical emergencies, but patients and doctors alike also use it as an auxiliary office, treatment room, and clinic. Doctors will send patients to the E.R. for penicillin shots; they also meet patients at the E.R. and then either send them home or "upstairs," as the rest of the hospital is known to the E.R. About 15 to 20 percent of the patients admitted to the hospital come through the E.R. Others of course come through the regular admitting office. Patients (especially indigents) often confuse the E.R. with a clinic and come in for regular non-urgent examinations and treatment. Some patients in California come to the E.R. to try to buy penicillin shots and drugs. We had a number of addicts then, too—perhaps not as many as now.

E.R. patients are of every age, every race, every walk of life, every socioeconomic background, and every medical and surgical condition possible. I soon came to the conclusion that one had never seen it all. There are always new surprises.

Patients are *not* seen on a first-come, first-served basis. They are seen on the basis of priority of need. People in shock and pain are seen first. People in life/death crisis situations have top treatment priority. Patients are charged minimal fees and are treated without payment if necessary.

Consultation when necessary is made with attending staff specialists on rotation basis; Dr. John Madden, attending chief of the E.R. department; Dr. David Morgan, chief resident surgeon; and the patient's private physician, if he has one. Follow-up work is advised by the private physician or, lacking a private doctor, the patient is referred to a staff physician from the hospital's rotating list. Paper work—filling in forms, clinical histories, securing treatment permits and signatures, and so forth—is the responsibility of the nurses. Doctors are responsible for brief chart write-ups of physical findings, diagnosis, and description of treatment.

There is a definite hierarchy in the staff of the emergency room. Lab technicians on rotation from hospital central lab are autonomous, as are X-ray technicians, who are on rotation from upstairs central X-ray. Unlike some other hospitals where interns do lab work, here the lab work, including blood counts and urine analyses, is done by lab technicians. X-rays are taken by technicians and read by interns who get "stat" (immediate) help if necessary. The X-rays are read "dry" by the chief of radiology the next day, and the same day if required.

A chief E.R. nurse is in charge of nurses and nursing. She alternates with other chief nurses from upstairs, but in my time no other alternate chief nurse became a permanent member of the E.R. nursing staff. Two non-registered practical nurses or nurses' aides comprised the nursing staff. Nurses from upper floors were sometimes called in to help temporarily.

Nurses work in eight-hour shifts, but the E.R. chief nurse and other nurses on duty often work overtime or alternate with a nurse who is temporarily sent down from upstairs.

There are three interns, who spend three to four months on E.R. service during their internship. Ideally, there is a physician who works in the E.R. full time on a reputed "good salary basis." Interns generally finish and start their work on July 1. But since many interns come from Europe and may arrive here at any time of the year, and since the hospital needs doctors, they may begin interning on any date. Interns receive $75 per month, meals, laundry, and room. Interns and residents on duty, rotating through other services, are sometimes asked to help in the E.R. if things get hectic. Some "wanderers" like to come through the E.R. in spare time on their own. Interns do all the simple procedures, and some of the complicated ones—such as tendon repairs or fracture reductions—under supervision. Difficult complications are usually handled upstairs in the O.R. or on the medical service. E.R. interns are sometimes required to assist on the floors upstairs.

E.R. interns sometimes work twelve on and twelve off; sometimes twenty-four on and twelve or twenty-four off; and mostly twelve on and on call the other twelve. But they must cover the E.R., and their duty hours often overlap in all kinds of haphazard ways to provide this coverage. Mostly they are in and about the E.R. nearly all of the time during their three or four months of E.R. service.

These are the people—staff and otherwise—in and around the emergency room, and my impressions of them:

Jonas Quistle.   Chief hospital administrator, non-M.D. About fifty, short, squat, ruddy, fast-smiling, firm handshake; reminds me of a politician.

John Madden, M.D.   Chief of traumatics and chief of the E.R. service, about fifty-five years old. Trained in general and orthopedic surgery. Tall, husky, thinning hair, blue eyes. Very alert, speaks in one- or two-word grunts, all business and highly competent. Reputed to have a bad temper and looks it, but I never saw it in evidence.

Doesn't seem to be friendly with anybody. A sort of detached benevolent despot.

David Morgan, M.D.   Chief house physician in charge of E.R. and surgical residents and interns. American education. Completed surgical residency training. About thirty-two years old. Medium height, thin, slightly stooped, rimless eyeglasses, long face, light blue eyes and waspish Connecticut-Yankee look. Very dry sense of humor. Not talkative—has a fund of good knowledge, good judgment, and considerable patience. Appropriately authoritative, but quite democratic and never despotic. A totally responsible, dedicated and involved guy—patient-wise.

Ted Rubin, M.D.   Intern. Twenty-eight years old, foreign-trained, tall (6'3"), big-framed and too heavy (250 pounds), dark hair, light eyes. Fair knowledge, fair adaptability, likes medicine, especially E.R. work and psychiatry.

Bill Roger, M.D.   Intern. Twenty-seven years old, small, thin, wiry, American-trained, competent, reliable, energetic. Likes to joke and have fun, but difficult to really get to know. Despite "hail-fellow" surface, is mostly reserved and detached.

Kurt Waggoner, M.D.   Intern. Fifty years old, German-trained and recently emigrated here. Medium-sized, dark, husky, slow-moving, serious- and even intense-looking. Understands English but speaks in a very heavy accent. Reliable, hard worker, but seems to have marked medical lacunae.

Eugene Lazo, M.D.   The Silent One. About forty-five, regular E.R. working physician—not an intern. Hungarian-born and -trained. Big and rugged-looking with deep voice, which is seldom heard. Quite competent and fast-moving when necessary. Not present when I started.

Jean Logan, R.N.   Chief E.R. nurse. About thirty-five, dark, thin, pretty but not beautiful. Rather frosty and sarcastic manner, always maintaining dignity and authority. Paragon of organization, efficiency, and reliability, but often quite bitchy.

Betty Smith, R.N.   Logan's most frequent alternate. About twenty-eight, capable, but much slower than Logan. Not good-looking, but warm, rather sweet person who likes to chatter. Medium height, a bit bulky.

Liz.   Nurses' aide. Forty-five years old, tiny, capable quiet and patient. Darting eyes—takes it all in but says little.

Mary.   Nurses' aide. About sixty, white-haired, good-natured, very helpful, compliant, bright—learns very rapidly.

John O'Hara.   A big, husky, open-faced, good-humored city policeman; Logan's boyfriend and occasional E.R. visitor.

Chuck Grayson.   Principal ambulance driver.

Albert Smithson, M.D.   Chief OB-GYN resident and principal hospital wanderer. Thirty years old, tall, thin, dark hair, brown eyes. Big sex talker—preoccupied with breasts, legs, behinds—women—sexually, gynecologically, in all ways other than as total human beings and real people. Capable, good sense of humor; an excellent E.R. worker when he chooses to help.

Alvin Johnson, M.D. Chief of internal medicine. About sixty, tall, white-haired, big-framed—looks like Oliver Wendell Holmes—much dignity—a doctor's doctor type of doctor right out of Central Casting. Reserved but kindly, and seemingly knows his stuff.

Peter Hennesy, M.D. Assistant pathologist. About forty, thin, dark, tense, and obviously thoroughly involved in his work.

Morton Post, M.D. Chief of OB-GYN. Older man, whom I met only once. Has the reputation of a celebrity practice and very high fees.

Peter Davis, M.D. Plastic surgeon. Forty-five years old, thin, tall, Basil Rathbone looks, very cordial and reputedly very capable.

John Tracy, M.D. Chest surgeon. Fifty-five years old, small, heavy man—looks like Edward G. Robinson. Affable and authoritative. Morgan praises his technical ability.

Manfred Hauser, M.D. Neurosurgeon. Forty-eight or forty-nine years old, Ivy League manner and looks—seems like a pompous, pretentious ass, but has considerable prestige.

Jack Stamm, M.D. Chief of ophthalmology. Forty-eight years old, European background. Tall, thin, stooped, scholarly. Excellent surgical reputation, with special interest in corneal work.

Ralph Watkins, M.D. Head and neck surgeon. Sixty-five years old, a small, meek-looking man with good credentials and reputation in this highly specialized area. Originally an E.N.T. (ear, nose, throat) man.

William Aiken, M.D. E.N.T. man. Thirty-eight years old, medium-sized, husky, gruff; an outgoing guy completely lacking in pretense. Seems to be A-1 at his job.

Arthur Mankowitz, M.D. Psychiatrist. Early forties, Edinburgh graduate, a regular, earthy, capable, direct guy.

Dick Sheffield, D.D.S. A young man, seems bright, capable and dedicated to his work.

The doctors' E.R. language is usually freely loaded with scatological and "strong" terms and curses. This is especially true at times of stress. This talk becomes somewhat diluted and muted in the close presence of conscious women patients and the nurses. Nurses' language—at least as observed by the doctors—is somewhat stilted. Under pressure they may utter a "damn" or an "oh shoot!"

Conscious patients usually whisper and are very polite—almost reverential. Weeping and sounds of anguish are almost always inhibited and subdued and often followed by embarrassed apologies. There are stunning exceptions, however!

The emergency room complex occupied one large wing on the ground floor of the hospital. An ambulance alley and parking lot connected to this wing, as did a pedestrian entrance that functioned independently of the hospital main entrance. A broad corridor with two elevators opened through large swinging doors to the main body of the hospital. Four small side rooms (each containing two beds), a small blood and urine lab, and a large waiting room were situated on one side of the corridor. The other side consisted of a very large examining and treatment room connected by a door to a medium size X-ray room, a branch of the upstairs X-ray department. All rooms opened on the corridor and thus were only split seconds away from each other. The corridor elevators and swinging doors hooked the E.R. to all floors and sections of the hospital.

The emergency room was extremely well equipped. I don't have anything like a complete inventory, so what follows is a list of the things that stick out in my mind, either because they were most in use or for some other known or unknown odd reason.

Stationary Equipment

Two large and two small sinks with hot and cold running water.

Four examining and treatment tables, which are fully adjustable, up and down and tiltable, so that patients can be positioned flat, sitting, or standing on feet or head (for shock).

Fluoroscope and X-ray machines in E.R. auxiliary X-ray room.

Diverse lab equipment in E.R. auxiliary lab room, used mostly for typing and cross-matching blood for transfusions, and for urine analyses, blood counts, and blood and urine sugars.

Small Equipment

Every size and variety of hypodermic syringe, hypodermic needle, and ear syringe (rubber and metal for the high pressure needed to remove foreign bodies).

Levine tubes (long rubber tubes), and Levine tubes attached to rubber suction bulbs for stomach-pumping.

I.V. stands, bottles, plastic tubing, and nozzles for transfusing liquids through the vein.

Hard rubber airways, short, curved, hollow tubes that hold the tongue down and dip into oropharynx to prevent asphyxiation in unconscious patients (for example, epileptics).

Ear, nose, and throat examining sets.

Powerful spotlights for eye, ear, and nose examinations; also ophthalmoscopes and otoscopes.

Suction machines, for clearing pharynx, nose, or suture site of blood clots and other discharges.

Proctoscopes, for rectal exams and treatment, to help remove rectal foreign bodies.

Tracheotomy sets, consisting of knife, clamps, thread, and neck insertion tubes.

Thermometers, oral and rectal.

Sterile suture sets, consisting of: rubber gloves; small slit drape sheets (the slit exposes the laceration, while the rest of the sheet covers the surrounding area); talcum powder to make hands dry enough to slip easily into gloves; needle holders; needles of all varieties and sizes—curved with smooth edges, curved with cutting edges, and straight, from fairly large to very small ones which are fused to the end of the thread so that the needle diameter at the thread end need not be enlarged to accommodate a hole for the thread (these are called atraumatic needles and are used to minimize skin suture scars); glass tubes of sterile catgut and silk thread from #1 diameter to #4.

Bandage pads, sponges, pledgets, ribbons of all varieties, sizes, and shapes, including rolls of Ace-type elasticized bandages of every dimension.

Adhesive tape in all forms and sizes, including tubes of liquid adhesive.

Scotch tape of all sizes, ideal for holding face dressings.

Stethoscopes and sphygmomanometers (mercury and aneroid) for measuring blood pressure.

Electrocardiograph machines.

Swivel chairs of adjustable height.

Every variety and size of forceps and hemostat.

All varieties of common tools, such as saws, wire cutters, pliers, etc.

All kinds of metal, wood, and cage splints.

Powerful stand-up adjustable magnifying glasses, hand-held lenses, and eye-glass magnifiers.

All kinds of flashlights.

Toothache kits, containing gums, oil of clove filling, small forceps, etc.

Every variety of scalpel, knife, and scissors, including surgical, bandage, and tailor scissors.

Special gadgets to cut off finger rings and fish hook hubs and to drill holes in fingernails.

Urinary catheters, including simple catheters and Foley indwelling catheters for urinary retention and for comatose patients who can't urinate voluntarily.

Many other pieces of equipment, plus innovative gadgets constructed on the spot for unique conditions and situations.

Drugs

Snake and spider antivenom. Though I used these only

twice, they impressed me since I would never have used them at all in a New York hospital.

Luminal, phenobarbital, Seconal, Nembutal, and several other barbiturates, used for sedative and hypnotic effects.

Chloroform and ether, for use while treating dislocations and fractures.

Dilantin, used for starter doses in epilepsy.

Nitroglycerin, for angina pectoris.

Aspirin, Empirin, and codeine, for pain.

Demerol and morphine sulfate, for severe pain.

Coramine, caffeine sodium benzoate, adrenalin, and digitalis, used for heart conditions.

Picric acid and Metrazol, used as analeptics to bring patient out of drug-induced coma.

Mecural hydrin, used as a diuretic to activate the kidneys.

Mesantoin, to paint skin before extensive adhesive tapings in order to make tape removal less painful.

Antihistamines, including Benadryl and Pyrabenzamine, used in allergic reactions.

Aminophyllin, used mainly in bronchial asthma.

Adrenalin nasal packs, for nosebleeds.

Penicillin and all other antibiotics, for use against potential infection.

Tetanus antitoxin, anti–Welch-bacillus toxin, and antitoxins, for use against any possible variety of gas-producing bacilli.

Merthiolate, burnless iodine, Furacin, procaine ointment, and other antiseptics and unguents, including a small variety of surgical soaps.

Mineral oil, for lubricating.

I.V. (intravenous) fluids, including sterile NaCl, glucose, plasma, and plasmoid.

Oxygen tanks (and masks and catheters to administer O_2), for all kinds of conditions, including heart attacks, overdoses, asthmatic attacks, and acute alcoholism.

Fluorescein, to stain and detect corneal foreign bodies and abrasions.

Ear oils and medications of all kinds.

Ophthalmic procaine and other eye anesthetics, antibiotics of all kinds, and sterile NaCl in special bottles with nozzles attached, to wash out eyes.

Coffee, tea, orange juice, lollipops, and a constant variety of diverse foods, including whiskey.

Many other drugs that I do not recall now, twenty years later.

Treatment of patients who come into the emergency room usually involves one or more of the following procedures:

Suturing Lacerations

The area is shaved by the nurse except for eyebrows, which are never shaved (they may not grow back). The area is then scrubbed with surgical soap (if scrubbing would be extremely painful, the area is first locally anesthetized). The area lateral to the laceration is injected with procaine—only rarely is the laceration itself injected: this enhances possibility of infection. The laceration is draped. The doctor, wearing cap, mask, and gloves, ties vessels off if necessary, using catgut, and closes the skin wound using smallest needle feasible and thin silk (#3 on body, #1 on face). Sutures are placed to completely close wound with ample tension, but not too tightly, as this produces edema and excessive scarring. Patients are told to see their own doctor or to report to the clinic for suture removal in one week on body, four days on face. Suture site is dressed with Furacin. Patient is given injection of T.A.T. (after skin-testing to rule out allergy to horse serum) or tetanus booster plus intramuscular penicillin (half a million units) if wound has taken place under infectious conditions.

Removing Foreign Bodies from Eye

Wash with sterile saline, anesthetize with ophthalmic procaine solution (one drop in each eye). Evert lid and remove foreign body with sterile *wet* swab.

Removing Embedded Particles and Examining for Corneal Abrasions

Proceed as above, then stain with fluorescein, and flush fluorescein out. Particle and abrasion will remain stained. Spud out, using magnifying glass, attempting to obviate future rust ring. Apply ophthalmic antibiotic and dress with pressure pack so eyeball cannot move. Instruct patient to see ophthalmologist within twenty-four hours.

Nosebleeds

Anterior adrenalin packs if other measures have failed, and posterior adrenalin pack if bleeding still doesn't stop.

Check for elevated blood pressure and possibility of systemic problem.

Finger-Ring Removal

Wind thread around finger distal to ring, attempting to remove ring over threaded-down edema, using mineral oil as lubricant. If necessary, cut ring with ring-cutter—getting patient's written consent first.

Overdoses (Barbiturates) and Poisons

Analeptics (I.V. picric acid for light coma and I.V. Metrazol for deep coma) if patient is truly unconscious. Always do gastric lavage, putting antidote (e.g., milk for corrosives) in stomach before removing gastric tube. Tube through nose or mouth is optional. Lubricate tube with mineral oil. O_2 must not be given in deep coma, as it inhibits respiration.

Simple Surface Bleeding

Apply pressure directly on bleeding point.

Puncture Wounds and Splinters

Cleanse and give booster or T.A.T. after skin-testing for horse-serum allergy. If wound is complicated by possible tetanus or gas (Welch) bacilli, inoculate accordingly and consider possibility of incision and wide curretage. Cut clothes to remove splinters if necessary. Avoid suturing where possible.

Fish Hooks

Cut hub and push through in direction of barb. If hook is too deep, incise down to barb and work loose. Give T.A.T. and penicillin plus Furacin dressing.

Nail Crush

Relieve hematoma pressure with nail driller.

Ankle Sprains

Rule out fracture with clinical exam (inspection, test mobility, etc.) and X-ray. Tape with figure-eight elasticized bandage. Advise cold compresses first few days, warmth later on.

Dislocations

Inject with Novocain and work the necessary manipulations. Strap tightly and refer for follow-up.

Fractures

Simple fractures must be splinted immediately. Heavy cardboard splints are best. Fractures can be reduced and cast only with attending physician present. Where possible, use local procaine for anesthesia rather than general anesthesia. Inject hematoma at site of fracture, draw up blood, and reinject with procaine. Must have follow-up. Compound fracture repairs are O.R. procedures.

Fractured jaws require dental and E.N.T. intervention.

Auto Accidents and Other Massive Physical Traumas

Examination for shock (blood-pressure fall of more than 20 mm. systolic), in which case urgent and immediate treatment is indicated—head down, I.V. fluids, M.S. (morphine sulfate) for pain. Proceed with total examination involving all systems: head, neck, spine, E.N.T., neurological, bones, abdominal organs, state of consciousness, response, etc. Use X-ray wherever necessary. Treat accordingly. Withhold M.S. in suspected head injury.

Burns

Must be treated locally and systemically. Ruling out shock is most important. If shock is present, must be treated immediately. Treat with I.V. fluids—as usual, plasmoid followed by whole blood as soon as type and cross-match is complete. *But*—a patient who has a cardiac condition must not be blood-flooded. Tilt head down if necessary and give M.S. or Demerol for pain. Debride dead skin from burn area and cover with moderately pressured Furacin dressing. Keep patient comfortably warm. Cortisone, antibiotics, T.A.T. prn.

Bronchial Asthma

Apply O_2 and give adrenalin I.M. Give I.V. aminophyllin if necessary, but inject very, very slowly.

Kidney and Gall Bladder Stones

Demerol for pain, but must differentiate from drug addiction and must be referred for follow-up. Addicts simulate gall stones, kidney stones, and everything else in the book.

Cellulitis, Infectious Streaks, Lymphangitis, Furnacles, and Carbuncles

Give antibiotics, advise wet dressings, and warn that follow-up is crucial.

C.V.A.

O_2 and airway if comatose, urinary catheterization prn, immediate consultation.

Urinary Retention

Catheterization and consultation.

Coronary Infarct

O_2, M.S., tourniquets on all limbs if heart failure is a complicating factor (also, diuretic if necessary to help drain off excessive lung fluid accumulated as result of failing heart). Nitroglycerin for angina (not for infarct), caffeine sodium benzoate, Coramine, and intracardiac injection of adrenalin only if patient is moribund (Cheyne-Stokes) or heart has already stopped. Consultation is always indicated.

Acute Abdomen

Think of appendicitis, perforated duodenal ulcer, ileitis, peritonitis. Get white count stat! Treat for pain and shock: M.S. and I.V. NaCl. Get consultation stat!

Hysteria

Placebo, comforting words, warm blanket, Luminal prn.

EMERGENCY ROOM
DIARY

Today a new doctor came on duty. He's about fifty years old, short, bulky, toothy, and very clumsy—all in all, rather sloppy looking, too. We were introduced. His name is Waggoner, and his English is four-fifths German. He's doing an internship so that he can get a license here in California. I can't resist and I ask him, and he tells me. Yes, he was a member of the Nazi party. Through no fault of his own and all the rest of the no-fault apologetic crap: he had to join or he couldn't practice, etc. Me, Ted Rubin—a Jew —I listen to all this politely, like I understand and accept it all. So there we are: me a Jew and him a Nazi making like a doctor, pretending we dig each other so nicely. It's disgusting. I don't mean him—I mean me. I ought to walk out or at least ignore him or something. Instead, I find I want to believe him, all the stuff about his not being able to help it and that he did no harm and all the rest of that garbage. God, how half-assed I am. Why don't I spit in his eye or something? Is it cowardice? I'm half his age and twice his size! Even as I write this, I begin to feel sorry for him. Me and this crazy self-effacing Jewish nobility of mine. Morgan wants me to help acquaint him with things. Instead of kicking his ass, I'll wind up mothering him. A Nazi, no less. It's unbelievable!

Waggoner couldn't have done too much damage—he's too dumb. But so were a lot of the other bastards who worked the gas chambers.

He really knows from shit, though. I wonder whether he had anything at all to do with medicine before he came here. They're so desperate for help in this place. How well did they check his credentials? Says he was a G.P. in a small town. This is impossible, because a practicing G.P. fifty years old is bound to know a great deal, and this guy is really out of it! He gave an asthmatic woman I.V. aminophyllin today in ten seconds flat. Also, he forgot to take the tourniquet off before injecting the stuff. This guy will kill somebody for sure if he's not watched!

We had eighty-eight cases today. A record for the week —so far. There are three of us, but I swear I saw seventy of the eighty-eight. I'm so tired I can't move. Funny, me calling them cases! Just a few months ago I made big lectures to myself to remember that *people* must never become *cases* if I'm ever to become a decent psychiatrist when I leave here.

I'm so tired I feel drugged. I'm nauseated from it—or from eating so damn much. These twenty-four-hour stints will kill me for sure. Not the work or the fatigue, but the food: the more tired I am, the more I eat. Christ, I'm up to 251. I've got to get myself impressed with the lunacy of this or I'll eat my way into an infarct for sure. Can't wait to begin psychiatry. But have to admit this E.R. work gives me a good feeling, too. No more hamburgers, though—I solemnly swear, as of tomorrow A.M. proper dieting stat!

It took Waggoner four hours to suture a leg laceration today. The woman was so stiff from lying in one spot she couldn't straighten up when we took her off the table. Trouble is, he's a perfectionist—and he's so clumsy he's almost a borderline paralytic. Quite a combination. It was a long cut—from her knee to her ankle—but no tendons, arteries, or complications. Should have taken half an hour at most. Four hours—I clocked him. Fifty-year-old Nazi—maybe he would have liked to butcher her instead. That's not nice. But, who's nice and why?

Today a sixty-year-old man came in with a huge prostate in severe urinary retention. His belly was as big as a nine-month pregnancy. I just couldn't pass the catheter. But I learned something—me, the would-be psychiatrist.

I called the urologist, Dr. Robert Jason, and he straightened me out—and the patient, too. I was all set for a cystotomy or something else fancy and complicated. But Dr.

Jason gave him some Seconal and 100 mg. of Demerol and put him in a side room for half an hour. He then had me pass the catheter, easy as pie. Just a little time, sedation, and relaxation make all the difference in the world. A good lesson that I won't forget!

Today I had a fight with Logan. It was an icy kind of undercover fight that looked like a controversial discussion on the surface. I would have liked it to break through, and frankly I'd feel better if I had yelled and really told her off. I wonder if she realized we had a fight at all. She never blew her cool. My self-effacement again (a fancy term for cowardice?). Anyway, I guess I'm still intimidated by authoritarian women, especially head nurses.

The issue: we had an overdose. There I go, sounding as calloused as Logan. Anyway, a woman came in, about thirty-five or forty years of age. Her breathing was shallow, pulse rapid and faint, blood pressure 70/30, deep reflexes and tendon jerks poor. The cop who brought her in found a bottle in her room with two 1½-grain Nembutals left in it. I gave her picric acid I.M. and then slowly injected Metrazol I.V. But first I passed a Levine tube by way of her nose and pumped her stomach. It was sloppy as hell getting the tube down, and that's when Logan sounded off. She chose to tell me then and there that people had a right to kill themselves. Furthermore, she said it was darned "inconsiderate" that they chose the overdose route, which is almost never effective and just makes a lot of work for people who are trying to help people who really deserve help. Imagine this bitch deciding that depressed people ought to choose a "gun or knife" or "at least jump out of a window—something sure." When like a jerk I asked, she was very happy to let me know that this was *exactly* what she felt and so did Dr. Madden. I should have told her off. Instead, I chose to try to rationally intellectualize her out of this lousy opinion of hers. I tried to explain that the woman may very much feel like living a few weeks or months from now—which would be impossible if she were already dead. But this bitch mechanic of a nurse persists. She says the woman will be back making "busy work" for all of us all of her life. I call her mechanic because she's calm, cool, collected, efficient, and really helpful as hell all through this miserable discussion. Actually, she's always this way, however much the rest of us sweat. Maybe since she has no heart, she has no passion, no sweat, or anything else. But as a machine she's one hell of a nurse—the rotten bitch! Why am I so mad? Do I see myself as the great and all-compassionate healer or something? Maybe I'm pissed off at the patient myself. There were three D.O.A.s today, two coronaries and one auto accident. The guy came in in three pieces and here this physically healthy woman is trying to knock herself off. But hell, there's no free choice in it. She's sick even if it doesn't show, and Logan be damned!

California must be the capital of the world for overdoses. We had five today—five! Thank God Logan was off, but I have to admit the work is a lot harder without her to help. Why do these kinds of considerations have to get in the way and spoil my pure hate? Will these Goddamned human inconsistencies plague me all my life? Logan is a mechanical monster that functions like a crack nurse.

Today the Nazi is gentle as hell with a little lost girl whose nose is bleeding. He's the only one who can get her to stop crying.

What shall I call it? Guilt? Conflict? Certainly a confusing experience.

They called me over to the employees' clinic to examine a few applicants for jobs.

One young would-be nurses' aide is one of the most beautiful girls I've ever seen. She's dazzling. To make matters more complicated, her breasts are fantastic. They're big, pink, white, high—I can picture them even now, tonight. And I'm supposed to examine them yet, for lumps. No physical would be complete without palpating the breasts. Notice, I wrote "the" breasts. Guess it makes it easier if I disassociate them from *her*. So I go ahead telling myself I'm a doctor. I don't know what that's supposed to mean, because frankly I like the feel of what my hands are feeling and the sight of what my eyes are seeing, and I don't like myself for feeling that way. What an insane conscience I have—a super superego—of which I am not proud. I've got to get it through my head that doctors are just plain people with a little medical knowledge.

A little humanity and a little humility—if you please!

This morning I found out from Roger that there is a $1,000 bonus automatically given to interns at the end of the year. Added to the $75 per month, the money thing becomes an altogether different matter. I was really astounded, because nobody said a word about this during my interviews, and of course none of it appears in our correspondence. This afternoon I checked with the front office and found out why. Mr. Quistle told me that the bonus money was only for English-speaking interns. He then corrected himself, and went on to tell me that it was for graduates of American med schools, to encourage them to work here. For several years now, the preponderance of interns have been foreign graduates who can hardly speak English. The son of a bitch went on to say that he realized that my school in Switzerland was excellent; that I was the "best intern," the most reliable in the hospital; and that since I am American (by birth, among other things), my English is perfect. *But,* "rules are rules," and there's nothing he can do about it.

I feel took! Discriminated against! Prejudiced against! Like a second-class citizen! I feel like saying fuck you, and walking out of this lousy place. Why the hell did I come here to California anyway? These dirty duplicitous sons of bitches.

Still, they never promised me a thing. They never promised, but they sure kept it a well-guarded secret. That oily son of a bitch, Quistle! But I'm sure this kind of thing is a board decision. There I go again, putting rationalizations in the way of just simple blind rage. Why do I have to trace what I feel down to the roots? I'm really pissed off and logic be damned! I hope Quistle and his board drop dead—stat!

Morgan says he never knew a thing about the $1,000 and that he will speak to Quistle. The guy I can't look at is

Roger. He is perfectly innocent, and he also is the guy who told me, and I can't stand the sight of him. There are suddenly two sides of the track here, and I am definitely on the shit-eating side. But Christ, it's true! Roger is at times a considerable goof-off, and I work my ass off—and yet he gets the thousand. I've got to get this notion of justice out of my head. It's a man-made thing, and chances are it doesn't exist in most quarters.

Speaking of justice, Logan's fiancé came around to visit her today. Wouldn't you know he's a cop? Name is John, and he actually seems like a big nice guy. I'm immediately prejudiced in favor of larger-sized people like myself. It's the little ones like Quistle that you can't trust at all. There I go, getting paranoid for a change—and here I am bitching about justice.

Morgan says it's a "dirty shame," and Quistle felt genuinely lousy about it, but no dice and no money. Screw them all. I want no part of this place. Get done here, then back to New York for sure. Is it possible they're anti-Semitic here? Who goes to foreign schools? Mostly Jews like myself, who can't get into American ones! But I've got to cut this out—I'm only eating up my own gut. Though you wouldn't know it from my weight—255 this A.M. At 6'3" and an oversized frame, I hide it well, but I can't fool my arteries. I must diet, stat! No question about it, I'm a food addict. Any nervousness, anger, fatigue, and I run to glut myself. I notice something else too—if I eat carbohydrates in the morning, I'm off to the races all day; if I lay off in the A.M., I seem to be able to exert better control all day. Night duty makes the whole thing go out of whack. With six meals and Cokes in between—over twenty-four hours— who wouldn't gain weight? Well, enough bitching. Like I said—screw Quistle and lay off food!

Morgan came in today and made a big spiel about six points: 1. vertical mattress sutures; 2. face sutures; 3. shaving eyebrows; 4. strapping patients onto the treatment table whatever their condition; 5. treating patients in shock first and stat; and 6. with head wounds, shave off hair and locate cut before putting wads of bandages on to hide the damage.

1. Use vertical mattress sutures whenever possible. In other than face lacerations, use #3 black silk. Too-tight sutures cause edema, and stitches will eat through the skin. Tell them to go to the clinic for silk out in seven days.

2. For face sutures, use atraumatic needles whenever possible. Make many small sutures in lieu of a few big ones. Plain, no vertical mattress here—just end-tip closure. With lipline lacerations, be especially careful to match lipline junctures perfectly. Silk should come out in three days, four days maximum, to minimize scarring.

3. Do not shave eyebrows, ever! Sometimes they don't grow back, and this can sure as shit lead to malpractice suits here in the sunny state of California. This goes for boys as well as girls. People are very conscious of their looks around here.

4. Last night (Roger was on duty with the Nazi—thank

God not me!) a drunken man rolled off the treatment table. He came in with a small occipital laceration and went out with a sutured forehead and a big hematoma on his upper right maxilla. If he has trouble breathing tonight, it's because he may have cracked a few right ribs, too (for which Morgan says there's nothing to be done anyway). Fortunately for the hospital, he was too drunk to know what he came in with and went out with. So: strap all patients down. Morgan says that he once saw a big, heavy woman roll off and fracture a hip and arm. I'm adequately impressed and will not forget this one!

5. If there is any suspicion at all of shock, especially in auto accidents, take blood pressures of all victims and treat those in shock first! Stat! Top priority! Any systolic B.P. under 80 in adults is pathognomonic, even if there seems to be no clammy sweating, etc. Set up arm I.V.—both arms, and legs too if necessary—with plasmoid until lab can type and cross-match, then switch to whole blood. Keep eye on B.P., especially in older people, so as not to flood and cause cardiac embarrassment and even failure. Hand-pump fluid in if shock is profound.

6. A little bleeder can pump a lot of blood and make loads of bandage red enough to look like massive hemorrhage. Both cops and bus attendants love to gauze up heads. Take it all off stat—the hair, too, if necessary—and find bleeding point and clamp off and suture. (I've already been surprised at least a dozen times when alarmingly blood-soaked bandages are removed to find how minor the wound can be. Have to remember to tell everyone I know that if cut, especially on head, don't wad up a bunch of bandages—just squeeze down right on bleeding point with small gauze pad.)

Morgan is O.K., very practical. Pity he had to dilute it with long speech about California being the hotbed of all kinds of malpractice suits. Can't blame him, though. I guess the fear of malpractice hits surgeons most of all. He went on about patients' waiver signatures, releases against medical advice, and all kinds of legal crap. I don't blame him, but I don't have to write it all out here, either!

I went out on the bus today, and I wish to hell I had never gone. Chuck Grayson, the ambulance driver, asked if I wanted to go along for the ride. I was going off duty for the day, so I figured what the hell—I'd go. No, that's not exactly true. The fact is I was sucked in by the heroics of the thing. Even that's not true; I went along so *I myself* could feel like a hero. Twenty-eight years old, and I'm still a big kid. I felt like Joe Air-Corps all the way there. The siren, me the doctor, the whole dumb bit. There was a steep hill out near Laurel Canyon. I kept picturing myself getting out of the bus and acting like Dr. Kildare while a big crowd stood in awe waiting for me to perform my miracles. No such thing happened. There was no crowd. No one was there except two kids about seventeen years old and their motorcycles. Chuck and the attendant did the work. I was strictly a spectator and, frankly, I felt like a complete amateur. These two crazy kids had been going up and down the hill full speed on the cycles. One had fallen off and was now lying on the ground, unable to move. (His friend, unhurt, had made the call.) We quickly established that his legs, arms, and neck were O.K., and he was fully conscious. The three of us figured him for a broken back, what level we couldn't tell. At that point I felt completely helpless. I had no idea how to get him into the bus. The truth is, I couldn't recall a thing about lifting anyone with a suspected spinal fracture. Fortunately, Chuck and his helper seemed to know just what to do, so I stood by while they slid him on to a hard board and into the bus. They had handled cycle accidents before. Christ, why do I get so down on myself when I find there's something I don't know and that I'm a novice after all? Why can't I be helpless at times? This grandiosity of mine is disgusting as hell. I've just got to develop some honest humility. I'm a beginner, and that's where it's going to be for a long time to come.

Morgan was there when we got back to the E.R., and happily he took charge. He positioned the kid on the table so as to effect the least pressure on his column and cord. He explained the rationale of the position, and I'll be damned if I understood him or remember a word of what he said. I was just too tired, and now I still have that deep worn-out feeling, even though I've slept about four hours.

This morning Morgan came down from the O.R. looking like hell. He had just assisted Manfred Hauser, the neurosurgeon, on the motorcycle accident. The kid is going to be paraplegic. Just like that. Morgan had to get it off his chest, and he told me that Hauser—the big Hollywood-type neurosurgical star, with all the best *American* credentials—had fucked it up completely. Morgan said that it was truly unbelievable, that he'd never seen such lousy surgery in his life. What's more, it could have been all right

—it wasn't even a difficult case. He'd never operated with Hauser before, and suspects that this is a guy whose reputation is based on credentials and published papers. According to Morgan, he's "practically hysterical" at the table. Morgan swears the son of a bitch cut the cord. This seventeen-year-old kid is going to sit in a wheelchair the rest of his life, and no one in his family will ever know why.

I feel terrible about this. (All I've done is go out to get the kid from that hill and I already have a big vested interest.) But I've got to admit that at the same time I'm feeling lousy, I'm full of rage again over that $1,000. And Jesus, I must be a real bastard, because in the middle of it all, I feel good, too. I'm *glad* that that no-good all-American s.o.b. surgeon graduated from only the best American schools. Morgan had mentioned that to me, and he seemed so surprised that a man with such A-1 American credentials could fuck up so royally. Well, good for Morgan—he can go to hell, too!

This seems to be the week for lousy medicine. We had a room full of patients, and Waggoner really pulled a lulu. He was pumping plasma into this woman who came in off the road pretty banged up. I was busy suturing a drunk's head. (Someone must have bounced a bottle off him, because his scalp was like five tic-tac-toe boards gone crazy.) Anyway, I must have put a hundred sutures into him. My back was really breaking. I sat up and looked around and there was Waggoner, half dozing, pumping an empty bottle of air into this woman. The fluid had run out and he was going on like some broken record, rhythmically pumping away. I jumped up and got her unhooked. I wonder how much air she got—I thought for sure she'd die of an air embolus. But there must be a lot I don't know, because we put her in a side room and kept checking her all day, and she was perfectly O.K. except for her badly smashed leg. Waggoner looked as though he'd die of shock himself. Even he knew that he'd very nearly killed the woman. Roger and I didn't have the heart to chew his ass—the poor bastard looked so white and exhausted. It's really a Goddamned shame to put a fifty-year-old man through an intern routine. The state of California can't pass up the chance for cheap labor. Nazi or not, I'll be damned if we'll say anything to Morgan. Best thing is to try to make it a bit easier on the Nazi. He's really too old to be working this hard.

I visited the motorcycle kid upstairs today. We talked a while about nonsense and then I left. Neither of us said a word about the accident or his condition. I wonder if he knows.

Smithson, the OB-GYN resident, came snooping around today and then left. Roger tells me that this is the hospital cocksman. He makes these explorations looking for ass. Age, status, patient, nurse—none of that matters. This guy is a gun-notch collector and the hospital is his principal territory. His "factory" is one of the examining rooms over at the employees' clinic. It seems strange that his examining women all day doesn't lead to loss of sexual interest. Maybe not so strange. His screwing is probably just as impersonal as his examinations. There are a lot of beautiful babes around here; California seems to breed them. I can still picture that nurses' aide. Say, do I secretly envy this free-wheeling fucker?

Chuck brought in a sailor today, about twenty-two, twenty-three years old. They found him and a dead girl in a completely wrecked car in a ravine off Mandeville Canyon. They may have been there for days. He's still alive—physiologically and technically, that is.

He's unconscious. Deeper reflexes are poor, pupillary responses are poor. He has a chest full of gunk. He has a huge occipital hematoma and a large laceration, also a fractured upper left humerus (simple) and compound fractures of both tibias. About two inches of jagged bone are sticking out of the skin of both lower legs, one-third up from his ankles. His heart sounds O.K., and there's no overt evidence of any abdominal organ injury. He's undoubtedly got a severe skull fracture.

I sutured the laceration and we immediately had several consults on him: neurological, orthopedic, and complete medical (with Dr. Alvin Johnson, the internist). They decided on a tracheotomy and traction and wet sterile bandages for his legs. We gave him T.A.T., Welch bacillus antitox, I.V.d him with electrolytes and antibiotics, and will try to keep his chest sucked out through the trache tube. He's too sick for any possible large intervention. We're going to keep him in the E.R. side room. He'll come apart if we move him, and if he's in the side room we can all look in on him from time to time.

I've heard of people living like vegetables this way for years. This is a strong young guy—who knows?

The sailor's parents came in today. His mother tried to talk to him. She didn't seem to understand that he couldn't hear her. I wonder how the dead girl's folks feel.

We were jammed today, absolutely jammed. Only forty-five patients, but they must have had a meeting and decided to all come at the same time. In the middle of all this they wheel in a thirteen-year-old girl who is in no obvious distress, so we leave her covered up on the stretcher in the hall. I repeat, this girl is thirteen, and she looks thirteen. She is not one of these prematurely highly developed kids.

We finally cleaned out the place and got to her. Under the cover, between her thighs, is a perfectly healthy baby girl, cord intact. Since the cord is attached, there is no question at all that this is her baby. But the girl swears she doesn't know how this happened. Was never "fat" or "anything," never menstruated in her life "yet," never had labor pains, and had no idea she was going to have a baby. She doesn't seem at all crazy and speaks in a completely intelligible way. I remember a class in psychiatry in which the prof described cases like this occurring among primitive and also highly disturbed people. He said that inevitably the girl's father turns out to be the culprit. But this girl is neither primitive nor visibly disturbed (though I admit my psychiatric expertise is notably lacking). Anyway, we cut the cord and sent her up to Smithson's department.

About two hours later her mother came in, a well-dressed, articulate, middle-aged woman. Either she was pulling the greatest act in the world or this kid must have been wearing the tightest girdle in the world. She was clearly frightened, with absolutely no idea why her daughter was here. (This all happened in the E.R., before we sent her on upstairs to OB to see the kid—I mean kids.) Well, we sat her down and told her gently as possible that she was a grandmother. She very nearly fainted! She turned white and wet and looked shocky as hell. Then she got hysterical and began to scream—I mean scream: "Kill the baby!" "Please, doctor, kill the baby!" "My husband is going to kill me!" "Please kill us both!"

She kept on yelling this way terribly agitated—and me the future head doctor nearly shit in my pants from fright. I guess I can add hysterical mothers to the list of other kinds of women that intimidate me. Kurt of all people ran over and gave her a big shot of I.M. something. Later on he told me it was distilled water—he swore it—and we put her in a side room where she actually slept for two hours. When she got up, she made us all swear to help her give the baby up for adoption, which we did, and then she finally went up to see her family.

Just before I left the E.R. tonight, she came in with her monster husband. He looks like a lamb. They were all smiles and told us to forget the adoption nonsense. "We love our daughter and granddaughter, and we are the happiest people in the world."

California must be a great place for psychiatric practice.

I did a twenty-four yesterday. Was it yesterday? I know where I am, but I feel disoriented in time. Here it is, 7 A.M., and I'm so tired I feel like dying, but at the same time I

can't sleep. I used to hear people talk about being too tired
to sleep and now I know what they meant. Roger tells me
he takes 1½ grains of Seconal now and then. That's another
thing I heard—that there are loads of barbiturate and Dex
addicts among M.D.s, who depend on the stuff for sharp
A.M. awakenings. I can see how it starts—severe fatigue,
sleep interruptions—it's all a bad scene toward which I in-
tend to make no move at all. If I drop dead from being
awake, so be it!

Chances are more likely that it will be from acute indi-
gestion, though. I don't even want to weigh myself any
more. I just have got to lay off the chow. This feeling that
it keeps me awake is pure illusion anyway—I think. In
between five full meals over the last twenty-four hours, I
actually had two malteds, four Cokes, two hamburgers, and
half a bacon and tomato sandwich some idiot left loose in
the E.R. I really have to stop this, because I swear I'm beginning to get extrasystoles from all this bloat. Therefore, I
here and now put this oath to myself in writing: I eat like
a normal human being starting right now, and a small
normal human being at that!

Christ, what psychiatric syndrome is this, writing ritual-
istic notes to myself? Some day I will have to tell an
analyst this yet? Right now I'm too tired to give a damn.

Today I learned—in detail—about how not to break
round suture needles. Morgan insisted on giving us a long
lecture on this, a subject to which there is no substance.
Simply put, you do not put the needle holder too close to
the thread end of the needle, since this is the needle's weak-

est point. When you push through the skin, place the holder near the pointed section. Big deal. Now, what the hell was this about? An exertion of authority? Is Morgan getting tight-assed? Is Quistle trying to save up money so he can bribe American graduates into slaving here for a bonus of maybe $1,050?

He also told us that Levine tubes will go down the throat more easily—less gag reflex action—if they are real cold. Logan promised to keep some on ice, even if this does upset the obsessive scheme of her place.

Smith is such a hell of a nice woman—Mary and Liz, the nurses' aides, too. But Logan is one awful bitch. She really believes she owns this place. In a way, I guess she does, since she stays on while crew after crew of us leave. I suppose Morgan, Quistle, and Madden know this too, because they treat her royally. They never *tell* her anything. They *ask* her, and she refuses them half the time, and they take it. I guess they don't want to make waves. A crack E.R. charge nurse must be hell to replace, so they have to keep the Logan machine happy.

When I got back from lunch today, the place was empty except for Logan, Smith, and Mary. I asked where all the guys were. Logan said that they were all in one of the side rooms watching Madden treat a private patient. She couldn't understand why, because all he was doing was splinting a cracked clavicle.

I understood why as soon as I went into the room. Must have been ten guys there, and at least eight were from upstairs. News really travels fast. Madden never got so much attention for treating a simple fracture in his life. His patient had the most beautiful knockers in the world. She immediately displaced the nurses' aide in my breast-fantasy collection. With the figure-eight T-splint holding her shoulders back, her breasts reminded me of navy twin twenty-mm. AA guns. She didn't mind in the least. She was "sick," wasn't she? She had the A-1 rationalization for showing off what she got with perfect impunity.

It wasn't supposed to happen, but I got called last night, and it was the worst ever. The whole crew of us was there. The place was jumping all night. But that wasn't the bad part.

Another butane tank had exploded in a trailer in one of those camps off the coast highway.

I knew what it was even before they brought the guy in. Thank God there was only one this time. It's the smell. I don't know if it's the butane or the awful smell of charred skin that makes it bad, or both. The smell is terrible, the worst. I don't think I'll ever really get it out of my head. After working around butane burn cases, everyone else begins to get this stink, too. No amount of showering or shaving lotion seems to get rid of it. It just has to dissipate by itself, and that takes days. Maybe all this is in my head, but I don't think so. I've seen Roger go around for a week afterward sniffing at himself. I guess this is one for which there are no inoculations. Roger told me they inoculate students against all kinds of possible future contacts all through med school in the U.S. I wonder if Smithson got his for V.D. (There I go with the American thing again.

Hits me at the strangest times. Actually, it's a very good idea, and I'm surprised we never got any kind of immunization shots in Lausanne.)

I've seen about fifteen butane burns so far—all trailers—including three D.O.A.s and four little kids. This is the first time I've had one who came in alone, the sole victim of a butane accident. The reason is simple: the guy, about thirty or thirty-five, is single and living alone. In a lousy way this is the only thing good about it, because he has no chance at all. He is by far the worst case I've seen who remained alive after the explosion. As with the other butanes (already I'm calling people things like butanes—but everyone else does around here, too; still, I've got to guard against this) his skin and clothes, that is, what was left of both of them, seemed fused together. I had a hell of a time cutting him out of it all. Large pieces of skin came away in my forceps. It didn't matter, because I had to debride all of it anyway. The guy was fully conscious the whole time and felt nothing, I guess because of the shock and M.S. we gave him. After all this, he actually asked for a cigarette—smoking probably kicked it off in the first place. Even Logan relented, the guy was so pitiful. We moved the O_2 into the alcove and let him smoke. That's the crazy thing: he was horribly burned—over more than four-fifths of his body, a good deal of it third-degree depth charring—and yet his face and mind were completely intact. (And this despite being in shock—his B.P. was already way down, because with that kind of loss of skin there's nothing to hold fluids in. I remember my derm prof, who used to like to brag that the skin was the largest and most important organ in the body.) This articulate clearheadedness despite extensive and deep injury seems to be characteristic of exploding-gas burns—I asked Morgan, and that's what he said. Anyway, we had a screen in front of his chin, and from the way he talked you could tell the poor guy didn't know he had lost so much of himself. We did two cut-downs and pumped T.A.T., fluids, plasmoid, antibiotics, cortisone— the whole soup—into him. None of which is going to help a damn. It will all just ooze out through his capillaries. It must have taken me and the Kraut two hours to debride him—we both did it as quickly and gently as possible—but as I said, he didn't feel it anyway. We then swathed him in sterile Furacin wrappings. I remember my prof telling us about aluminum, Vaseline, Furacin, and nothing at all— just a light, warm, sterile cradle. I wonder if any of it helps. We also put in a Foley catheter, and this really got to me (castration anxiety?), because he was pretty badly burned in that area too.

By the time we sent him upstairs he had fallen peacefully asleep—still with no idea of his condition.

Just now, before I left, his girlfriend came in. We told her as gently as possible. Of course, she hadn't seen him yet, and I could tell she didn't believe a word. Isn't this called "denial"? I can hardly blame her. She asked about grafts, and we just shrugged it off. Jesus, it's hard to tell people that things are hopeless. Of course he'll never make it to the graft stage.

I went up to see the butane case today and he's in a deep coma, definitely moribund.

Our sailor boy is still alive but shows no sign of recognition or anything else that resembles consciousness. Roger has pretty much taken over his I.V. electrolyte stuff. I have to admit the American schools are better on lab work. But *anyone* can look up a lab-test value—physical diagnosis, *clinical medicine,* is really the thing!

The burn case died. He never knew he would. He never asked, and nobody ever told him how bad off he was.

No change in the sailor! I guess I have a special feeling about him—I think the whole E.R. does. He is, after all, our only continued patient. Everyone else comes and goes. I don't see how he can make it, though—there's absolutely no evidence of neuro improvement in any area.

We keep changing his leg dressing, but the smell is terrible. Not exactly gangrenous, but very bad, nevertheless. There I go with my delicate nose again. But I'm not the only one. He used to get a lot of visitors but, aside from his parents, they've tapered off. I don't know whether this is because of hopelessness or the smell or both. The smell is pretty unbearable—we've tried everything, but it comes through and hangs on. But his mother sits there and doesn't seem to mind a thing. She talks to him, quite normally, as if he's going to respond any time now if one just waits a bit. Is this denial, too, or love, or what? I guess it's entirely human to deny reality when the chips fall this way.

I lost five pounds—down to 250! I've got to watch it though. I know myself. I'll think I'm doing so great I'll drift on to a binge again. Though I don't look it (I hope),

I'm still forty to fifty pounds overweight.

This A.M. there was some talk about transferring the sailor to a naval hospital, because this kind of care can turn out to be a very long haul. In the afternoon three (three, no less) navy doctors came to see him and decided he couldn't be moved. He will stay here and the U.S.N. will foot the bills. We could see the expression on these all-American faces when they went into Sailor's room. The stink really hit them. This endears him to us all the more. Why don't we like the military even in the form of doctors? With me it's the American/Swiss thing again. If I continue with this paranoia, I'll need help long before I get to analytic training.

Today was real quiet. I couldn't believe it. I kept waiting for the proverbial shit to hit the fan. But aside from a few lacerations, it was the calm before the storm—with no storm. Was just thinking about the thousands of stitches I've made. Worst comes to worst, I'll make a hell of a tailor.

Anyway, I had a chance to read today—Karen Horney's *New Ways in Psychoanalysis*. I like her approach much more than the Freudian. Less faith, more clinical validity. Sounds more practical. Some attending internist, whose name I don't even know, came by and asked what I was reading. He sneered and made some snide horse's ass remark. I've noticed this fairly consistently. There is a deep and wide schism between the psych thing and all the other M.D.s. Who's afraid of whom, anyway?

Sailor's Foley came out and we had a hell of a time getting it back in. I guess it got deflated and slipped out. Why should it have been so hard? He's more than relaxed; he's unconscious. But maybe that's not true. Maybe there's spasm here and there, along the urinary tract anyway. We finally got it back in. Hell, let's face it—*I* got it back in. I'm getting pretty good at these tough little jobs, and I'll miss them when I leave here. But I can't help it. Psychiatry beckons. Anyway, the catheter is in and Sailor is making urine. His kidneys and, as a matter of fact, his whole vegetative system, are fine—but he just lies there, completely out of it. This guy is young and strong, so who knows? (There I go with my own denial routine—and a bit of wishful thinking thrown in.)

Sailor's mother is a lovely person, by the way. She's simple and nice. She says she just knows her son will be all right. I hope she's right. She nearly always brings us candy, fruit, and cake, which I need like a hole in the head. But I can't deny that the pig in me (all 253 pounds as of this A.M.) loves her for every morsel.

A terrible thing happened today.

Two days ago Madden admitted a man of about thirty-five with a simple Pott's fracture. He sent him upstairs, and that was the last I thought of him until today. At four o'clock this afternoon we got a call to send someone upstairs to look at this fellow because he was acting "funny" and the people upstairs were tied up elsewhere. I was elected and ran upstairs. He said that he had a pain in his chest and a funny feeling all over and trouble breathing,

but that now he was O.K. But while I watched him he suddenly turned absolutely pale, clutched his chest, and went
into Cheyne-Stokes respiration. Then, just like that, he
came out of it and seemed perfectly O.K. again. Just then
Madden came in, thank God, and I described what had
happened. Madden, who is perfectly calm in emergency
situations, got really agitated, and just then the patient
went into Cheyne-Stokes again. This time, before we even
got a stethoscope to his chest, he died. Just like that he was
dead. Madden told me that without doubt it was a pulmonary embolus lodged in the pulmonary bifurcation,
where it causes instant death. Imagine dying from a nothing little clot. This thing started with a simple fracture. It
circulated around, and got bigger and bigger, until it
couldn't get through and became a killer. Anticoagulants
would have prevented it, but on the other hand they can
cause bleeding and delay healing. When I read of pulmonary embolus in school it seemed so theoretical, and here an
otherwise healthy guy in his thirties is dead of it. Madden
said the guy had two kids. Jesus, how terrible. Madden was
really distraught. He paced up and down, saying that he
didn't know how he'd tell the guy's wife. On his way upstairs he saw her waiting to come up on a routine visit, and
he had to tell her that her husband died of a simple fracture.
God, I don't envy him. Of course we tried intracardiac
adrenalin and dry massage, which we knew was only a
symbolic gesture.

Since I've been in this crazy town for a while I'm no
longer shocked by goofy religions, neon signs advertising

life-ray treatments, buying blood-pressure readings on the street, Chinese herbalists, people trying to buy penicillin shots in the E.R. without physical exams, etc.

But to license murder is something else again. Maybe I'm being dramatic, but when they license some of these characters, this is just what they are doing, and I'm so naive I only *vaguely* believed it until last night—at 2 A.M., to be exact.

This Armenian family—about seven people, parents, uncle, aunt, and cousins—came in with the patient, a nice-looking guy, thirty-one years old, with a history of ulcerative colitis. This man looked terrible, absolutely white and bled out. His B.P. was 60/40 and going down before our eyes. His hemoglobin was only 4 gm., less than one-third of normal. We began to transfuse him with plasmoid immediately and typed and cross-matched him in minutes. We had him on whole blood, Vit K, and some new coagulatory drug that just came out—I can't remember the name—all literally inside of minutes. We also flat-plated his belly and applied tourniquets to his arms and legs and had him positioned almost on his head because his pressure was going down by the second. It took no great brain to see that he was bleeding to death.

Out in the waiting room Logan got the necessary signatures and the whole story. The guy was doing O.K., no colitis attack in several months. An uncle, who I guess was afraid to meet us and had gone on home, started the damage. It seems that they were all at a family gathering when he insisted that the patient, George Kasmanian, looked bad and should go to see his "doctor." His "doctor" happened to be a chiropractor whose specialty is high colonics (which involves a mechanical kind of high-power rectal flushing and enema—another modality to cure all ills I see advertised here). Everyone had drunk a little wine, but thought it was a good idea because George did look a little pale. George to this point had been hospitalized twice, no surgery, and was doing O.K. under treatment by Morey Katz, a reputable gastroenterologist over at Cedars. When they got George to the chiropractor and explained to him the nature of George's illness, he said he knew just what George needed: "a good cleaning out." After the high colonic, they went home and just about when they all got sober, George told them he was dying. He could tell from his previous attacks. He turned out to be absolutely right, because he died of massive frank lower bowel hemorrhage while they were evaluating him upstairs. I guess the surest way to kill someone who has ulcerative colitis is to open everything up with a big strong enema. We told the family in no uncertain terms, and I hope they crucify that son-of-a-bitch chiropractor. I wonder how the well-meaning uncle will feel. But I've already learned a bit about how people rationalize things to go on living with themselves. I'll bet this bastard high-colonic fuck manages to come off smelling like roses. California —this is a lousy state!

Before I left the E.R. the guy's family was going out. One woman looked absolutely crazy with grief—she must have been his mother, even though she looked forty-five or fifty at the most. The rest were practically carrying her. She seemed almost paralyzed. Somewhere I once saw a painting like this—Goya I think? Several people carrying a grief-stricken woman away from a battlefield tragedy or something else catastrophic.

Sailor is alive—no change.

They hate Mexicans here. Everybody's got to have some one to hate. Whom do the Mexicans hate? I rather thought Logan was treating Mexicans a little like children. This being patronizing is a special forte of hers. What an arrogant bitch! I hear the same prejudice applies to the Japanese, but as yet I've seen no evidence of it. I wonder how they feel about Jews? Guess they're busy enough with their own special minority hang-ups. Jesus, what makes people so crazy arrogant? It's like a disease that started somewhere way back and then just goes on from generation to generation with no rationale at all.

They've got their own special hates here, and they also have their own special diseases and problems, the bastards. I saw two examples today.

One fellow, twenty-six years old, came in who had been working in Tulare County up to two days ago.

He said he was feeling very sick, running fairly high temperatures and was having trouble breathing. Like the good European clinician that I am, I looked at his hands, and there on his right index finger was a punched-out crater that he said was a "hell of a funny kind of boil until it began to heal several days ago." I listened to his chest, getting more and more excited as I went on. He was full of rales, both lungs. His temp was 103°. Then I asked him the pathognomonic question, and there it was! Yes, he had, up to the time he came here, been hunting and skinning rabbits! Morgan fortuitously came in at the dramatic moment, looked the guy over, and announced, "Pneumonitis." I said, "Yes, but better put him on tetracycline—this guy has tularemia" (a form of bubonic plague, yet). I told him about the rabbits and the primary site on the finger. He looked, all the time marveling at the wonders of my brilliance—actually, I had read up on this in *La Suisse* not so long ago. Morgan said I could be right and we sent the guy to the county hospital. He said, to quote: "Ted, that was really a good one." But I could tell that he was impressed way beyond his simple statement, and so were all the rest of the E.R. folk. Times like this make me feel so good (what do the Freudians call it—"narcissistic supplies"?). With enough of these little boosts, maybe I could keep from eating!

But what is the whole business of diagnostic skill? Being open and alert to all possibilities is I guess vital, plus of course having the basic information to put together. Without the facts, there's just nothing there to jell. But it's more than that, too. The putting together part is the major thing, I think, the whole business of the right associations coming together at the same time. Why, what, how—the way the brain pumps out thoughts as the heart does blood fascinates me, and also makes me feel like a class-A ignoramus because I don't understand a thing about it. I wonder if this free-association thing and the meaning of dreams I've been reading in Freud really clues you in to as much as he says. Jesus, look at me here and now, only at the ass end of an internship, already full of enough arrogance to question Freud just because I had the luck to make a tricky diagnosis. Horney believes in the free-association bit, too, and she's quite pragmatic. As I read her stuff I see myself and everyone I know in every line. But some day they'll have rooms full of computers loaded with every bit of medical information possible. M.D.s will call a number and bang! the diagnosis and treatment will shoot back at them, eliminating the human factor altogether. That's where psychiatry will come in, because no machine can replace what goes

on between people. I can't help but think of the great placebo effect on that thirteen-year-old mother's mother. Suggestion is powerful stuff, but why? Does it touch off
something that's already there, loaded and waiting to be
touched off? Did she really want to stop the hysterics and
sleep? How many so-called cures have actually taken place
this way? Who knows?

Today was all used up with asthmatic attacks, coronaries, splinters, sore throats (here in California nobody gives
a shit whether or not a condition is an emergency—they
come to the E.R. and use it as a clinic), a fractured finger,
two overdoses. (We haven't lost an overdose yet—they go
home or go upstairs and then leave. They really should go
to psychiatrists. Logan gets them to say they won't do it
again, someone comes for them, and they usually go home
smiling. Maybe they've really accomplished what they
wanted with the gesture, and feel better now for having
done it.) There were also, of course, innumerable lacerations and suturings. Why am I trying to be so blasé? Still
hung over from my diagnostic heroics? Truth is, it all
gives me a hell of a lot of satisfaction. There really is no
such thing as E.R. scut work.

This evening the second California thing came in: a
snakebite. Now that's something I'll bet the guys in New
York have never treated! Anyway, this guy came in from
the desert via the coast highway. This was a rattlesnake
bite, and his leg was literally as big as a balloon. I don't
think I've ever seen anything quite like it, not even in elephantiasis, or so-called milk leg, either. This leg may not
be as big, but it is nevertheless huge and absolutely tight,
red, and angry looking, with an ugly red streak already
going up the calf—cellutitis starting, I guess. We tourni-

queted, incised, cleaned out, and shot him full of everything. We also I.V.d fluids, because he will sure as shit go
into shock. Thus I got the chance to use the antivenom kit.
We finally sent him upstairs, a pretty sick twenty-eight-
year-old guy. He already had a good deal of groin adenitis.
Systemically he seemed O.K. so far. Heart, lungs, sensorium—reflexes all O.K. Very brave or crazy, because he
seemed comfortable and confident. His temperature was
already 101.5° when we sent him up.

Morgan then chose to give us a lecture on the spot on
California wild life—snakes and spiders, that is. He's O.K.,
really knows his stuff. I guess I'm impressed with esoteric
knowledge but here, of course, this stuff is not so esoteric
—it actually happens.

Essence of Morgan's talk:

1. All snakebites have to be taken with extreme seriousness. Venomous snakes show their stuff very quickly.
Swelling, lymphadenitis, cellulitis, and pain come on
very fast. Systemic response may be slower—elevated
temperature and shock. Treatment: intermittent tourni-
queting, incision, T.A.T., antibiotics, cortisone prn, and
set up I.V. so as not to waste time. Many patients will
become comatose and tracheotomy, Foley, and full take-
over may be necessary. Much depends on age and general physical condition. Morgan took the opportunity to
remind us to skin-test everyone who gets any kind of
horse serum, including T.A.T. He's told us this at least a
hundred times, but I can't blame him. He's seen some
pretty awful anaphylactic reactions and has heard of even
worse California malpractice suits.

2. Female black widow spiders hang around garbage cans in sunny California. The male is harmless. Only females have red hourglass design on their bellies. Here a bite can kill an infant, and it can make an adult very sick. Treat as with snakebites.

3. Scorpion bites, Morgan imagines are like snakebites but isn't sure, and suggested Roger look it up and clue us in.

4. Tarantulas are virtually harmless.

5. V.D. is on the upgrade out in desert areas. He threw this in to be funny, but we were too tired to laugh.

Antroll! That's California, too. Back home I never knew this Goddamned stuff existed, and here kids eat it like it's candy. What's the matter with these fucking parents? We get an average of two or three ant powder cases a day. Maybe this is where native Californians first get the idea of overdose.

I saw a really pathetic case today, though. A woman, young, early twenties, swallowed a load of ammonia. She burnt hell out of herself. We lavaged her with milk and sodium bicarbonate. Sent her upstairs and called William Aiken, the E.N.T. man. The thing he has to try to prevent is esophageal stricture. What a mess for both of them! I think the procedure is to keep passing graduated bougies so that the esophagus doesn't close up. Drinking ammonia is a particularly miserable thing to do to oneself —psychiatrically it undoubtedly comes under the heading of severe self-hate. Imagine not being able to eat via the mouth again! Seems to me I remember a case of a man who accidentally swallowed lye and had to be fed through a gastric fistula for the rest of his life. Me with my oral cravings—all this hits particularly hard.

Sailor is the same, but the smell is worse. The face masks we wear don't help at all. It's fantastic, but his mother quietly sits there as if she doesn't notice a thing. If she doesn't stop bringing us home-made cookies, she's going to kill me for sure. Is this what's known as "projection"? Tomorrow I go to a lecture on suicide given by a psychiatrist who is an attending here, a Dr. Arthur Mankowitz. Sounds Jewish. Hope it's brilliant! I guess I'm slightly chauvinistic myself.

Couldn't tell whether this Witz guy was Jewish or not, but it was a damned good lecture. I was the only one from the E.R. there. Considering the number of suicide attempts we see, we should have all been there, but of course the others want no part of that "head stuff," to quote Roger. Makes me happy to see how solid and pragmatic an aspect of psychiatry can be.

SUICIDE ESSENTIALS: IMPORTANT TO
REMEMBER FOR THE FUTURE

1. Anxiety hysterics kill themselves to get even with other people, as "vindictive triumph." Much rage here! Usually gestures, but often successful. Overdose is most common route. If alcohol preceded barbiturates, the barbits may be potentiated into unpredicted and fatal effect by knocking off brain vital centers. Cut wrists are also

common with anxiety hysterics. They have the misbegotten notion that they will be there after they're dead to
have the pleasure of seeing everyone feeling sorry and
guilty. They often leave dramatic notes, to let everyone
know. If these people get into a good relationship with
someone they think "cares," especially a therapist, they
may keep selves from suiciding. (The same is true of
depressives.)

2. Depressives do it out of pain—they can't tolerate
their self-hate and depression. They usually do it when
they're getting better and depression has lifted enough
so that they have the energy to formulate a plan and to
carry it out. They mean business! The main routes are
gunshot, cooking gas, carbon-monoxide poisoning, and
jumping out of windows.

3. Chronic self-haters with few or no overt symptoms
do it through "accidental" car crashes, drowning, fall-
ing out of windows, ski mishaps, etc.

4. Schizophrenics who commit suicide also have much
self-hate, and are trying to kill part of self hoping the
other part will live or that some kind of rebirth will take
place. They often hear voices (auditory hallucinations)
that tell them to jump in front of trains, etc. This is the
most bizarre group. They often choose ways that will
obliterate the self as much as possible. Common routes
here: hanging; jumping out of high buildings or in front
of trains; exploding self with bomb devices; cutting
throat; cutting off head (Mankowitz told us of one man
in a state hospital who was determined and wedged his
head in a swimming pool between the ladder and the side

of the pool in a way that made rescue impossible until it was too late); shotgun blast in mouth; hacking self to death; dynamite; etc.

All talk of suicide must be taken seriously. People who do it also talk it, though all people think it at times—mostly Mankowitz says as a symbol of having the freedom of doing with oneself as one wishes, as well as seeking freedom from cares and responsibility.

I wonder where the ammonia woman fit. Was going to ask him, but felt inhibited—self-effacement again, or maybe grandiosity. There I go, feeling I should know it all, even without clinical experience.

I tried to get the guys here involved in a discussion about suicide. Impossible! They just didn't want to know and didn't want to talk. What is this? Denial? Fear? Resistance? Or just simple lack of interest—if such a thing exists. Would love to get into some psychiatric discussions, but it doesn't seem possible around here. Will have to wait until I get to my psychiatric residency.

The whole crew of us did, however, get into a big discussion about of all things connective tissue. I took the unpopular—in fact, the only—position that blood and bone are connective tissue. True, I was being a smart ass, but it's also true that I believe blood and bone *are* connective tissue. How, after all, do you define connective tissue? Interstitial material interspersed with cellular materials, as opposed, let's say, to epithelial tissue, which consists of stacks of cells and nothing in between. The guys wouldn't buy it, but it's true:

Blood
interstitial tissue = plasma
cells = erythrocytes, thrombocytes, leucocytes

Bone
interstitial tissue = calcium
cells = osteocytes

I guess I was showing off. I like to stick into these guys' craws that a future psychiatrist—a foreign graduate, yet —knows some basic medicine. The $1,000 is still sticking in my gut. I just can't let go of things, I guess.

But the truth is, the stuff really interests me, and I'm going to miss it when I begin psychiatry. Maybe I can come around here once in a while or maintain some connection in some way. But I suspect I'm pipe-dreaming. Just not enough lives to live and something's got to give!

Buzz-saw accidents are also a common California disease. I've seen a number of hacked-off fingers and one entire hand. The handless guy was in agony, but he was lucky enough to be with someone who used a belt for a tourniquet. Great combination: people here love woodwork and hate themselves. This morning an elderly man came in minus a finger (left index, from second joint); and a cop came in a few minutes later with the finger in a handkerchief. The old man didn't seem the least perturbed. We called Morgan, figuring we could maybe sew it back on. He decided to throw it away. Funny, seeing a finger thrown into the trash can. Maybe a crack hand surgeon could have done something with it, but the nearest one is a guy in San Francisco.

Anyway, this reminded me of a beaut I saw about a week ago. I didn't write about it here—as a matter of fact, I'd really forgotten all about it until now—selective repression? Maybe, because this is only the second time I can remember that something like this got me sick, and I don't even begin to know why. A man came in with his right arm—lateral version, maybe four inches down from the shoulder—laid open to the bone. Muscles, tendons, nerves, vessels, everything cleanly bisected right down to the bone. He wasn't bleeding too much. We clamped off a few small bleeders and the wound was completely dry in no time. After M.S. and the usual penicillin, etc. routine, we sent him upstairs, where he will be Madden's private patient. It seems an axe flew off a friend's handle and cleaved him this way. The thing about it, though, is how sick it made me. I've already rotated through all services here, I've seen every mess possible in surgery and plenty in the E.R., too, and this *cleanly dissected* cross-section of an arm made me feel real woozy. I'm ashamed to say I could hardly look at it. Why? I think it was *because* it was so clean—dry and clean, laid out like meat in a butcher shop. I think if it had been all blood and gore—like most massive injuries —it wouldn't have bothered me at all. I *know* it wouldn't have, because God knows I've had those experiences. If the guy was dead, it wouldn't bother me. I've dissected the arm and everything else on my own cadaver in school, and the only thing that got to me was the smell of the formaldehyde. I can't really explain it—maybe the imposition of that meat store look on a live man gets to me. Maybe it's the reminder that underneath that skin of ours—*mine*—there's all this mechanical bone, tendon, nerves, raw stuff. I think we normally disassociate what goes on under the skin from ourselves and here, bang, I'm suddenly forced to make that association. This of course reminds me of the other time I got the same feeling. It was the first day in the dissection lab. Popoff had us all gathered about this dead man whom he hadn't yet filled up with formaldehyde. The poor guy was young, killed in an accident, and he hadn't been dead long enough to lose the human look. He really seemed like any one of us—at least I must have felt that way, because I soon felt lousy as hell. Popoff took a scalpel and with one brisk deep stroke lanced him open from sternum to pubis. He spread his incision and there the guy was laid open, with coils of intestine, liver, stomach, all of it clearly visible. Maybe what got to me was the mortality of it all. That's what we all are under our skins, a bunch of pipes and things that keep us going, and we are vulnerable as hell—but you don't know it when it's all covered up. Maybe that's why Popoff did it, to quickly remove any ethereal, spiritual feelings of immortality. In any case, it really rocked me. After that, I didn't think I could go through dissection, but I had no trouble at all. I never once, including now, identified myself or living people with cadavers. The gray, hard look and feel of them helped dehumanize them, and I guess that lousy formaldehyde did, too. This guy with the arm, though, was very much alive—alive and conscious.

Injuries and comeuppances seem to come in swarms. It's as though somebody was out there today carrying a sign saying, *This Is Dislocation Day.*

Unbelievable, but we had three dislocations today, and also a smashed patella (which is not a dislocation, but it's a bit related anyway). Madden got that one upstairs quick where he will undoubtedly charge a fortune to remove the thing. Can't put it together—it felt like gravel, and must be in ten pieces. I hear Madden gets two, three hundred bucks for a half-hour's work. Real money is undoubtedly manufactured by the bushel in the surgical specialties—but they can have it.

The three dislocations: Knee (patella business again); jaw; shoulder. I did O.K. with the knee, straightened out the leg and eased the patella back into place. Ligaments are undoubtedly torn. I wrapped the leg in figure-eight Ace, gave her a cane (middle-aged woman), and told her to report to orthoclinic on Friday.

The jaw: Guy was eating and the thing went out of whack and he couldn't close his mouth. I couldn't either. We called Dick Sheffield, our only dental attending. He closed it and explained how, but I'll be damned if I understood. I know I'll have to call him again if another whacked-out jaw walks in.

The shoulder: This was my second comeuppance. I've done these before, and I did everything I was supposed to. Injected the Novocain, positioned the old man just right, all of it according to Hoyle, and all I produced was a hell of a lot of pain for the poor guy. The thing just wouldn't snap back into place. When I finally got Morgan, it took him all of about two seconds, and I swear he did exactly what I did. I always thought I was pretty good at these kinds of manipulations. I've set about ten Colles's and four Pott's—a couple of clavicles, too—but now I'm beginning to wonder. Maybe I don't have the surgical touch after all. Though I still feel that if I didn't go into psychiatry I'd surely choose surgery. But the final indignity was still to come.

The surgical assistant resident was tied up and they asked me to *please* come upstairs and pass a Levine tube on a private gastrectomy. I could tell this guy was a ballbreaker the minute I walked into his room. He had this supercilious look and managed to say a few things that conveyed the idea that he was big stuff and I was the local bellhop. What really came through was that he was pissed off that his own private doctor ("who is charging me plenty") was not there to shove down the tube. I wanted this thing to go smoothly, so I made the nurse get a tray of ice, in which I put the tube. This delay further irritated the patient, and the miserable s.o.b. began to give me the business about "slow-poking around" and "creeping Jesus" and so forth. Trying to maintain some little dignity—and not much was left because I lost most of it downstairs with Morgan and my shoulder dislocation—I dipped the tube in mineral oil and put too much on the fucking thing, so that it kept slipping when I tried to shove it down his nose. All in all, though, it couldn't have been more than two minutes, when I finally had it going down. Well, he started to gag, as everyone does initially, and he grabbed the thing, pulled it out, and pushed me away, yelling that I was a clumsy s.o.b., etc., and to get out. I did just that, real fast—because I knew that if I had stayed another second I'd have clobbered him for sure. I can easily see why the s.o.b. is getting his stomach out. I guess I'm so put down and shocked because I really do feel that doctors are part of a select priesthood or something and ought to be treated with special respect. A couple more guys like this, and I should get over that notion pretty quick. What I'm really disappointed about, though, is how personally I take this kind of thing. This strikes me as a pretty shitty psychiatric attitude. What if a psychotic patient chews me out? Do I sit in judgment on him? Do I want to clobber him? Or do I want to try to understand and help him? Right now I guess all these feelings are true—I have them all at the same time. Maybe that's why a personal analysis is necessary, but that's still a long way off. Besides, this bastard upstairs isn't psychotic. But how do I know? Maybe he is, and what's the difference anyway? Right now he's a very sick guy and nervous as hell, so temporarily anyway, he's slightly out of his head. Which still doesn't really help my self-esteem (Karen Horney's word; my pride is really wounded—more Horney), and I will go on being vulnerable as hell if I continue to harbor all these illusions about doctors' knowing it all, instant success, etc. So what I tell myself here is step down, fellow, get off the pedestal and expect anything at any time at all—that's what the E.R., and I suspect medicine, the world, and just plain living, is all about.

Christ, being alive is tenuous as hell. It's very scary to give it any thought at all.

We had six D.O.A.s today. The one that hit me most was this young guy who dropped on a tennis court. He came in here, took three deep breaths and that was it. I pounded down on his sternum and did a dry heart massage. Also gave him Coramine and intracardiac adrenalin, but he never took another breath. Couldn't be more than thirty.

Cerebral aneurysm? Infarct? I don't know. All I know is that he was innocently playing tennis a few hours ago, and now he's dead. The guy was obviously an athlete, in great condition, and it did nothing at all for him. I swear I'm going to lose weight and lay off cholesterol. But all this really just amounts to magical incantations, because this fellow didn't have an ounce of fat on him. Nevertheless, I better watch it. I'm young but not that young, and I still eat like a Goddamned pig.

To top it off, Sailor gave us quite a scare today: his temp suddenly shot way the hell up. We got all kinds of consultations and nobody came up with anything at all. Of course, bronchopneumonia was most on our minds, but thank God his lungs are perfectly clear. This itself is remarkable, even though we keep sucking out his trache and move him as much as we can; which is no small problem with his pus-y, cracked legs. Well, we alcohol-sponged him, which didn't help. Then we ice-packed him, and his temp finally came down. I sat watching him for about an hour. He's like an organic factory that has a certain amount of input (I.V.s) and output (urine, etc.). What goes on in his head? Anything at all? There he is, cut off from us all—does this mean he is completely cut off from himself, too? Is he psychologically dead, or what? We've done no E.E.G.s or even spinal taps—absolutely nothing fancy or extensive. Before I left I looked in on him again, and I'm happy to write that his temp was still fairly low (100.5°, to be exact).

Sailor's temp is normal. Nobody seems to know why it went up and why it is now down. Maybe something to do with his brain injury. Anyway, he's O.K. now—O.K., that is, relative to his position yesterday.

Today is one of those unusual days for L.A., especially this time of the year. It's actually brisk out. This reminds me of Lausanne so much I can almost taste it. I really miss Switzerland terribly. Sometimes it hits me hard as hell, like an attack of some kind, and this is one of those "attack" days.

I think this whole Furacin thing on burns is a waste. Worse than that, I think it creates pain. It strikes me we use it just to make us feel that we're doing something useful. Had this woman with a severe leg burn today—boiling coffee. Quite an extensive area, and quite a burn. Even with 100 mg. of Demerol—and she didn't weigh more than 110 pounds—I could tell she was still in agony. I could also tell that the Furacin didn't relieve her a bit, and I hold its curative powers much in doubt. This woman's grimaces were awful. She'd just let out the smallest kind of suppressed yell once in a while when I was debriding, and then she'd look terribly embarrassed. Meanwhile, the tears were running down her face. I told her in so many words to cry and scream out if she felt like it, but this only led to her apologizing. More and more I'm convinced that the silent ones are no more brave nor courageous than the screamers. They're just more inhibited, and may have confused notions as to what constitutes courage. As a matter of fact, I think it's their self-effacement that keeps them from really letting go and sounding off and getting some relief. How do I know this—from what great clinical source? From a number of people I've seen here and, let's face it, mostly from myself. About two years ago I had a hell of a leg burn in Lausanne (European bathtub side faucet), and as I was being treated I kept apologizing for making any sound at all—and I know that I was in agony and didn't feel at all brave or any of that crap. Jesus Christ, why do we have to apologize for living even when we're in great pain and really need help?

Anyway, I wonder more and more about the wisdom of all this tissue-cleansing and sterile wrappings in burn cases. In Logan's words, it's probably all "busy work"—and God knows we have enough to do without wasting time hurting patients. Maybe, considering my very minuscule experience, this is arrogance on my part, but I have the very strong (rigid, inflexible, prejudiced?) notion that I'm right. I'll bet some sharp detail man sold Madden on the idea. If I get up enough guts I'm going to ask. But this may not be easy—I suspect it comes under the heading of not apologizing for having doubts, which is a function of being alive and showing it! Not at all easy, somehow.

The Kraut is *not* dumb—I have to give the devil his due. He's really picked things up fast, and he's completely reliable and tries very hard. But weren't they all this way at the crematoria, too? Is it an automatic kind of thing? Just point them in the right direction, and it's O.K. If they happen to get turned in the wrong direction, then, like the Golem or Frankenstein's monster, they just grind everything up. But he really seems human enough, and I wish he didn't, or that he weren't German, or that he hadn't been a Nazi, or that he hadn't told me. When you get down to it, actually get down to it, I can easily see why reality—

real reality with all its inconsistencies, and especially our
inconsistent feelings—is so bloody hard to take. I can see
why people push things down out of awareness. I've been
thinking of this unconscious thing. We don't go about re-
membering everything at the same time; we have a memory bank and can call most facts or feelings up when we
need them. And there are things that are so abhorrent that
we put them down, lose touch with them, but they sit
there and cause trouble. We do this because we live in a
culture (Horney) that tells us what we should and
shouldn't accept *vis à vis* ourselves and the rest of the world.
Thus perhaps we develop too much repression, too much
unconscious, and in a way lose or deaden a good part of
ourselves. Is the whole unconscious thing then a perversion
of the memory device? Do we pervert the process of putting things aside until we need them by putting *much too
much* aside, especially feelings like—I'll be damned: what
comes to me now, and I don't like it at all but there it is,
is that I actually am beginning to like that fucking Kraut.
Enough analysis—it makes me too Goddamned anxious
and I won't be able to sleep and all this will surely wind
up in a great eating binge. Food—why is it always food?
Orality? What's orality? To gather substance, to feel more
substantial? To push down things I don't want to face,
maybe? Enough. I better sack out while I can.

Paid Dick Sheffield back last night. Last night? Again
I feel disjointed about time. Anyway, 2 a.m. yesterday—
today, rather, I guess. His patient came in bleeding like a
stuck pig from a tooth he'd extracted earlier—yesterday, I
guess. (I'm getting more and more disoriented in time

—some kind of early senile degeneration, maybe? Wonder how a guy in Sailor's condition must feel if and when he regains consciousness.) Anyway, it's pretty amazing how much bleeding a tooth socket can do. Reminded me how a woman can bleed to death when any placenta is left behind. All the bleeding goes on under the placenta, and here it was all going on under the clot in the socket (second molar). I guess the trouble with this kind of clot is that it isn't really tightly formed and puts no pressure on the bleeding point. Having already had this experience about ten times made me a bit of a genius. But the truth is I only reminded myself of all this after I tried stopping the bleeding without first removing the clot. Then I forceped out the clot—just like a dentist—and a load of old and fresh blood followed. I cleaned with sterile swabs and packed with Gelfoam, and that had no effect at all: she bled worse than ever. Then I remembered what my father used to do when people came into his drugstore with these things. I made like Walter Mitty and had Mary get me a tea bag. The patient clamped down on it for about half an hour, and it worked. When I took the bag out the socket was bone dry. The astringent effect of the tannic acid in tea is almost as powerful as silver nitrate, which I don't care to use in the mouth.

But the thing is, I hadn't remembered the tea bag thing until that minute. With all the others I treated and all through the years generally I'd have sworn I never even knew about "tea-bag antibleeding therapy." How come I recalled it this A.M.? Necessity? The girl, twenty-two years old, was very pretty and altogether a nice person—was that it? Wonders, miracles, and mysteries of the half-assed mind—I just don't know.

We all went upstairs to see an interesting case today. A woman, twenty-eight, gave birth to her second baby three days ago. All she had was a whiff of gas during the delivery; she was nowhere near fully unconscious. But she *is* unconscious now, and has been completely out since the delivery. She just lies there, showing absolutely no response to pain, light, noise, pressure, touch, etc. Reflexes are diminished considerably but are discernible. Reminds me a hell of a lot of Sailor, but of course she's sustained no trauma or head injury of any kind. Her husband and parents say she's always been perfectly healthy; her history is totally negative for all systems. So there she lies, all tubed up, input and output, the same human vegetative factory Sailor has become. She's had every conceivable consultation, and nobody has come up with anything the least bit helpful, let alone definitive. Differential diagnosis has included: diabetic coma (ruled out—I could have told them that. I've seen about a dozen so far, half when I was on medicine, half on E.R. Anyway, she's had absolutely no trace of acetone, elevated blood sugar, etc.); cerebral neoplasm (no evidence whatsoever to support this one); cerebral embolus connected to delivery (no evidence); cerebral aneurism (happens in postpartums, but no evidence here—there are just no real neurological signs present to support any kind of intracranial mess); anesthetic allergic dyscrasia (pure bull, and everyone knew it at once). They finally settled for a diagnosis that reads: "Acute and severe electrolyte imbalance associated with clinical trauma of pregnancy possibly due to anaphylactic response." This last one is Alvin Johnson's contribution and also sounds like crap—fancy internal medicine crap in this case. In any case, it makes everyone happier, because it enables them to do something. They are now in the process of "balancing her electrolytes." The assistant resident on internal medicine is busy running up and back to the lab making all kinds of titrations and arranging her NaCl, calcium, potassium, etc. I.V.s accordingly. Now we've got Sailor and this woman on a big electrolyte watch—though with Sailor it's just control and with her it's supposed to be therapeutic. Thank God this is one job that never fell on me. I think it's a lot of nonsense—after two days of it there's been no change at all. Besides which, this lab work leaves me cold—though I do admit this feeling may be associated with my lack of know-how in this area. Horney does say that arrogance covers up fear—you can add ignorance to that list, too.

Speaking of arrogance and ignorance, I had quite a mishmosh of dreams last night. Seems that I made some big pronouncements, and immediately everyone knew just what to do with Sailor and L.U.P. (as the unconscious Lady Upstairs is known in the E.R. now). I was waving a baton, like leading an orchestra, and everyone was treating the two of them according to my baton wavings. Then the whole staff turned into an orchestra, which I continued to lead, and L.U.P. and Sailor danced with each other all over the place. I woke up just as Madden handed me a check for $10,000. Now that I think of it, there was something else, too. There was something about me suturing Sailor's and L.U.P.'s dressing gowns together. I guess I've linked them in my mind. But, my God, what an omnipotent picture I have of myself—me leading the band! Well, if a dream is any kind of wish-fulfillment, at least this one indicates that I do want them to get well. But, me the band leader—the all-time healer! It's slightly grandiose and very embarrassing.

I went up to see L.U.P. today, and she hasn't changed an iota despite the heavy electrolyte routine. Why does it piss me off so? Is it because in med school biochemistry always worried me the most? In any case, it's very easy to be critical of the internists, but what do I have to offer that's better? I guess it's the helplessness thing again. I expect medicine to have all the answers and 100 percent therapeutic success and it's never going to be that way at all! Smithson came into the room when I was there and made some kind of vulgar remark. He's really a coarse, oily son of a bitch. Is this what psychologists call "displacement"?

Today I took off for two hours for my final residency interview over at the V.A. There were eight of us, and after it was over they showed us around the place. Some of the buildings seem quite modern, but others are pretty bad. Some of the patients there looked extremely deteriorated, and the surroundings are just plain lousy. Hard benches in a big empty gray ward, and these people just sitting around all day, looking pale and blank and doing nothing. They told us these were "backward cases" or "chronic patients" (every business has its labels). A few have actually been there for forty years. I thought this was true only of state hospitals, but the V.A. also has these people that nobody comes to see any more. Our guide told us that at first there are visitors but they gradually dwindle off. I thought of Sailor and L.U.P. I was also surprised to see a women's building, which should be no surprise at all since there have been women in military service, expecially during World War II: WACS, WAVES, and nurses. The "Female Building" is a vast improvement over the men's side of things. It's bright, warm-looking, and even home-like. I can't believe that disturbed men are any less appreciative of nice surroundings than disturbed women. I also can't believe that gray crummy surroundings don't make people more depressed, however out of it they seem. It's a crazy world, all right, and obviously a cruel one, too.

Later on I spoke to the guy who took us around, a third-year resident. He said the attendings and teaching program are excellent and the variety of "clinical entities" is vast, so why get hung up on physical surroundings? But it is a rather bleak place. Crazy, but the whole time I was there I kept thinking of the E.R. here. The E.R. seems so bright and lively by comparison; this place seemed like Zombieland.

The interview went O.K. The guy was really very nice, extremely gentle, understanding and at the same time managing to get a lot of personal info out of me. But when he asked me how I liked my internship, I went on and on about the E.R. I hope I didn't foul it up. I mean I hope he didn't get the idea that medicine and the E.R. kind of thing interests me more than psychiatry. Am I projecting? No, not really—the truth is I like them both, and psych is my decisive thing for the future.

Actually, what is it about the E.R. that I like so much? I work my ass off, I'm chronically tired—maybe that's part

of it: some kind of martyred "feeling good" that comes
from working to exhaustion. The hard-work ethic? I
don't think that's it. But I must say the feeling of having
put in a hell of a lot of physical work (and so much of the
E.R. is just that) makes for a sort of inner restfulness that
I never felt from hours of studying, however hard it was.
But the E.R. offers more than that, too. There's the team-
work, almost a family kind of thing—a small, all in all
very good, unit and a deep sense of belonging. The heroics,
the challenge—it's life itself all brought down to a micro-
cosm in which we, the doctors, play the central role. Speak
of "narcissistic gratification"—what possibly can beat it?
Quick evaluations, quick decisions, treatment, and immediate visible results—one way or the other—except for
cases like Sailor. Maybe it's the sense of adventure, waiting
for the unexpected. Maybe it's also the way the E.R. puts
a certain value on life: it clues you in fast and repeatedly
to the fact that life is pretty damn tenuous. This also makes
it all feel that much more valuable. What can make a person feel more worthwhile than fighting to save someone's
life? (It sounds melodramatic as hell, but it's true—except
for about 80 percent of the cases, which are splinters and
sutures.) There's nothing subtle about it—instant gratification in the most important work possible! I guess it's
the antithesis of boredom, a young man's dream come true.

On the other hand I had two cases today—two people
who died—who make all this sound like just plain bullshit.

One guy came in off a golf course—popular game
around here. He was maybe sixty years old, with a small
potbelly, and so cyanotic he looked like he'd been dipped
in blue ink. I could tell right away that it was a coronary.

Gave M.S., O_2, the works, but we never even got him upstairs. Must have been massive, because he lasted about ten minutes and all of our heroics couldn't bring him back. His wife, a nice elderly woman, came in about ten minutes later. She kept repeating, "My life is over, my life is over—forty years and my life is over." No hysterics, quiet, but she looked awful. Here are two people who, I take it, lived together for forty years, and now this guy dies in an E.R. he never even heard of—and she's supposed to go on alone. This whole life thing seems pointless as hell. And that's the way it is lately with me, up and down, shit to shinola—manic depressive, I suppose, or maybe just hypomanic, I hope.

The other one was a head injury. For a minute I thought we had another Sailor. Twenty-five years old and off the coast highway, but unlike Sailor there wasn't a mark on him, not a scratch. This poor guy took two breaths and just died. There wasn't a thing we could do. He had been in one of those small sports convertibles and it turned over, so we assume it was his head, but this is pure conjecture. Maybe a subdural hematoma or hemorrhage, or maybe even a broken leg, but nothing visible—nothing on the surface, not a scratch, *nothing!* They'll try to get a post on him. Logan thinks it's legally mandatory in this kind of case. Frankly, I don't care. Subdural? Broken leg? Coronary? What's the difference—dead is dead, and I can't see how knowing why will seriously add to our clinical knowledge. Besides which, what has all this got to do with psychiatry anyway? Well, at least no more D.O.A.s, paraplegics, and all the rest at the V.A. What's with me? Do I identify with patients who are close to my age? Like it shouldn't happen to them—too young, not fair! Am I looking for justice again? In any case, to hell with little open cars, and I don't want to know a thing about that post even if they do it here.

I guess everyone doesn't get *exactly* the same treatment, though this is what we would all like to believe. A famous actor came in with a fish hook in his palm. I'd never seen or heard of him. He must have achieved his fame while I was in Switzerland. So it was easy for me to be objective and to work the miracle cure. But everyone else just couldn't do enough for this guy. Logan was particularly disgusting. If the rest weren't fawning all over him, she would have gotten down on her knees and kissed his ass for sure. They were so solicitous it was unbelievable. Worst of all, Logan actually got his autograph, which he had no trouble giving even with his wounded right hand. I guess I'm disappointed in her: the bitch is human after all, it just takes celebrity status to get past her freeze.

Roger bumped into Peter Hennesy, the assistant pathologist, in the dining room. The young guy in the open car had a massive brain injury right at the base of his skull —and there wasn't a single outside mark. Could it be from the impact of brain against skull? Frankly, what's the difference anyway?

Just had a revelation: could I be trying to get myself to dislike medicine, this place, the whole works, and build up a load of cynicism so as to make it easier to leave? I've got to cut that. If that is in fact what I'm doing, it's cheap and self-destructive. I really don't know.

Maybe my revelation was valid. Like they say in the book, a real emotional insight. In any case, I feel better.

Today I received a detailed schedule of the program at the V.A. Funny, because I still haven't been accepted. I hope I am, because the program looks very good. There's going to be a hell of a lot of reading and much to learn. Funny, how often I've been a freshman. Just about catching on to something and off to the next move and beginning all over again. Psychiatry does seem that way, inasmuch as it seems so divorced from everything I've experienced up to this point. Yet I can't believe that premed, med school, and interning serve no purpose in the psychiatric scheme of things. I hope the powers that be know something and that medical training is not something just for the M.D. title or for the greater glories of the A.M.A. Yet all of these experiences—even here in the E.R. —must certainly contribute to a maturation process, to making decisions and to taking on responsibilities. But I'm not at all sure. What if all this time had been spent taking all kinds of social science and psychology courses, as psychologists do? What is all this ruminating about anyway? I guess I'm anticipating missing this lousy place. Here I am feeling pretty good about myself and my ability to do this kind of work, and bang! Just like that I'm going to take myself out of it and become what Roger calls a "talk doctor." Still, I have no doubt at all about doing it. What pushes me in that direction? My own problems, challenge, curiosity, grandiosity? Why would psychiatry be more grandiose or glorious than surgery? The intellectual implications—part of the Jewish strong-in-the-head glory mystique? I hear that most psychiatrists are Jews. Surgery is the real Air Corps of medicine. Maybe it's because I feel that psychiatry deals with the whole person, the real person. Besides, so many people with somatic problems turn out to have neurotic difficulties. This means that so many doctors must function like amateur psychiatrists, so why not become a professional? But if I didn't do psychiatry I would surely be a surgeon, and in surgery one deals with real somatic lesions. Truth is, I don't know, and the hell with it! I'm here now and I'm going to try to be fully here and enjoy it. In other words, the hell with psychiatry for the time being. I'll get to it soon enough, and then I'll do it for a lifetime.

I've been reading about conflict, and it just occurred to me that maybe I've been in the middle of one: psychiatry vs. medicine! Another insight? I don't know. I want psychiatry. I know that. The hell of it is, I want medicine, too, and I think I've been trying to blind myself to that. Jesus, is this what life is always going to be about, giving up things I love? Is this what choice and decisions are all about? A process of elimination because life is so fucking finite? Horney says that conflict creates anxiety. I have been anxious as hell, but mostly I've been too busy and too tired to feel it. But I am eating like a horse, and that with me is sure as shit a sign of anxiety. Maybe the trouble is that I've been trying to hold down my feelings about surgery. But what if I let myself feel the full blast of my conflict—how does that help? Yet, I suppose this is what psychiatry is all about, or psychoanalysis, anyway. If a thing is handled on a conscious level, then it isn't relegated to the unconscious, where it sits like a huge abscess causing all kinds of trouble. So? Is my abscess lanced? I freely admit more than that; I even accept that I like medical work. More than that, I even love it! But I still suspect that admission and acceptance are not enough. Giving it up is not going to be so easy, and eventually—as a matter of fact, in the not so distant future—I've got to do just that. Before long, things will be the reverse of what they are now. Now I work in the E.R. and I read psychiatry when I can. Some day (am I still inadvertently putting it off with this "some day" stuff?) I will be doing psychiatry and reading medicine. It's hard for me to visualize being an amateur doctor. My whole life has been geared to this thing ever since I can remember. But I suspect (wishful thinking? could be, but may well be true, nonetheless) that once I begin to work with psychiatric patients, things will settle into place. O.K. Let's face it, Rubin, you are a greedy guy. You eat too much and you also want to have the best of several worlds all at the same time. Neither will work, so come off both once and for all—here and now!

Jesus! Speaking of conflicts, Waggoner has asked me to his house. This guy has a wife and kids. Why I never thought he had I don't know. It just didn't occur to me. He's at the beginning of his internship, I'm at the end, and he treats me as a sort of professor, which is embarrassing as hell and which is neither here nor there. I just couldn't do it! I really feel that life ought to be a forgive and forget thing—otherwise the whole human condition will always be a hopeless mess. But I'm just not big enough for it. I think, in my guts, I really believe there is no such thing as willfully "bad" or "criminal" people. People who kill other people (Hitler and Nazis included) are sick and need help. Human pathology is pathology, whatever form it takes, and it needs human acceptance, understanding, and treatment. It's so easy to accept our saints, and so hard to accept our monsters—and our own personal monstrous characteristics, too. But with all this highfalutin philosophizing and psychologizing, in my guts I still hate these German fuckers and can't rise above these feelings of mine. Anyway, I told him no. Not in so many words, but in my usual self-effacing half-assed way. I made use of his lack of English to say no in a way that was definitely no, but which made the reasons unintelligible. Here is this guy, who is a pitiful kind of character, who may have been sucked into the Nazi thing because of his own shit-eating self-effacement—because he was afraid to say no. He is hardly the stormtrooper type! And here I am, and this is the way it is. I just can't rise above myself and, lousy as it seems, I still see him as a Nazi and I just can't eat at his table in his home and be part of all that that implies. This is my season for conflicts. Let's face it, the human condition is a pretty grim business. How the hell are we ever going to learn to really communicate?

Sailor's legs stink terribly. Thank God (whom I swear I don't believe in, but whose name I can't seem to do without), his temperature is normal and apparently stabilized.

Alvin Johnson sent a forty-year-old woman in today who had a pain in her chest and left arm. She looked O.K., no dyspnea, no cyanosis, chest clear. She said she'd had the pain off and on for several hours and when she called her

internist (Johnson), he told her he'd meet her at the E.R.
When I went over her, the pain was completely gone. Johnson came in, did an E.K.G., and then showed us the trac-
ing in one of the examining rooms. No question, she's
having a posterior branch occlusion, inverted T-wave,
the works! Johnson says this is an extremely anxious
woman who has a long, intensive history of hypochondriasis. He says that she won't make it. Her infarct may not
be so bad—the next several days will tell the story of how
much progression and damage there will be—but "her
anxiety will kill her." He suggested that I, because of my
psychiatric interest, go up and visit her now and then if I
get the chance. Then he sent her upstairs to medicine.

Her name is Mrs. James. She's getting M.S., O_2, constant attention, the works—which she really doesn't understand, because she says she feels fine. She looks fine,
too. I visited her, told her not to talk, just to wiggle her index finger in reply to my questions. All seems odd as
hell, because clinically she looks just fine. But E.K.G.s
don't lie, and this one ain't normal. Later on I saw Johnson
in the hall, and he told me that he thinks the thing is not
extending, but the trick is for her not to blow another one
in the next couple of weeks. I asked him if the E.K.G.
could be wrong and he said it could, but in her case it
isn't. He has a whole kaboodle of E.K.G.s on her because
of her hypochondriasis, and comparison to her old ones
shows definite damage. "Her own worst fears finally have
come true." He says that after thirty years of practice he's
almost beginning to believe that people can scare or wish
themselves into one of these things. I wonder.

Had a beaut of a diabetic coma today. The guy (age fifty-five) was wearing a metal tag saying that he was a diabetic, so the diagnosis was no trick. Since he was hot and dry, not cold and clammy, I knew it was coma and not insulin shock. We really broke our asses with this one —I.V., glucose to soak up the excess insulin we loaded him with, running up and back on lab tests, the works. We finally sent him upstairs and I left word with the new intern on med to call me if and when he came out of it. Meanwhile, the family sent in a private M.D. I never heard of. This guy really looked bad.

Anyway, before I left tonight I got the call and went up. The guy was fully conscious and looked just fine, like nothing had ever happened at all. I asked him if he remembered passing out, and he said "only vaguely." He conspiratorially confided in me, because "my wife and Dr. Green would kill me if they knew," that he'd eaten about two quarts of ice cream before it happened. He said he just couldn't stand all "the fucking control" any more and had to do something about it. Now that he's got it out of his system he'll be good for another ten years. Who says I'm not learning a little bit of psych here and there? This sounds like rebellion against Horney's inner coercions or shoulds—*n'est-ce pas?*

Also saw Mrs. James today. Johnson is allowing her to talk. She wanted reassurance that she was doing O.K., and I reassured her. Which wasn't hard considering how well she feels and looks. Her E.K.G. looks like she's stabilized, too. I just don't see this big anxiety in her that Johnson talks about. I'm glad, because she seems like a very nice person.

By the way, I've eaten nothing but protein for the last two days, and I don't know how long I can keep it up. I've got nothing but sympathy for the diabetic guy upstairs. A carrot is beginning to look like caviar to me. In any case, I must have pissed out five gallons of urine—this protein diet is real good to dry you out. Trouble is I know I'll gather it all back up again.

They put air conditioners in the windows today, and all they did was make a draft—until someone realized you're supposed to keep the doors closed, which is a pain in the ass. We had them put one in Sailor's room which we set on low so that he doesn't get cold. Hope to hell it helps the smell. I swear I dream about that smell, and I don't think I'll ever forget it. Thank God (God again, for a change) that we've had no butane cases lately.

Went up to spend a while with Mrs. James today. I guess this anxiety thing intrigues me. She's off O_2 and is doing just fine, though she did seem a bit more apprehensive than she had up to now. Is this my suggestibility or fact? It's hard to be objective in a thing like this. Her E.K.G. remains static, which is just fine at this point. She told me she has three kids, eight, fifteen and seventeen, and can't wait to get home.

I told Morgan all this, and he said that Johnson has a lot of clinical experience for which there are no theoretical substitutes. I respect this, too. We then got into a conversation, or was it an argument—Morgan never raises his voice, but he can be quietly firm. I said that we seem to get about ten male infarcts to one female infarct, and he agreed. But we differed as to etiology. He feels that this is purely hormonal. Estrogens block cholesterol plaque formation in the arteries, etc. To prove his point he says that most coronary disease in women occurs after menopause, when they are minus their "estrogen protection." I don't disagree with him, but took the position that men are more under the gun in our society than women are and this produces pretty destructive pressures and a good deal of anxiety. The whole manliness–bring-home-the-bacon–success thing certainly doesn't make for a relaxed psychology or physiology. I reminded him of the extraordinarily high coronary rate among doctors. He says that he's very wary of statistical logic and that I'm too much influenced by "psychiatric considerations." I don't really believe that's true. I think he's prejudiced by his knowing that I'm going into psychiatry.

Speaking of female heart lesions, today I saw a terribly tragic case, a real Goddamned crime.

This thirty-two-year-old, very pretty and very pregnant (last trimester—about seventh month) Catholic woman came in. She was in acute heart failure and could hardly breathe. She's had repeated attacks of rheumatic fever (I still remember from somewhere "licks the joints and bites the heart") since age eight or nine. That's why she moved to southern California from Michigan three years ago, but despite the warm weather she's still had joint attacks (fewer sore throats, though). Not only does she have chest fluid, cardiac asthma, the works, but I can percuss her heart all over her chest, it's so Goddamned enlarged. The mitril thrill is almost over to her lower sternum, and she has a mitril insufficiency that makes the loudest murmur I ever heard. She's digitalized, but she just has no more cardiac reserve left. This is her fourth pregnancy. How she survived the other three is impossible to say. She's told me she's been a service case here and a patient of the medical clinic since she arrived in California. She had her last baby two years ago and Dr. Post (our chief of OB-GYN) wanted to tie her tubes off (which should have been done after her first pregnancy) but she refused on religious grounds. We sent her up as a service case. I just don't see how she can make it! What can I say, except that people are primitive, crazy, cruel, self-hating, self-destructive, sucked in by religious vested interests that are impersonal and inhuman. Here's a clear-cut case of danger to the mother's life, making sterilization utterly justifiable legally, morally, religiously. But what do you do with a woman who's been indoctrinated since birth and is terrified of giving up her reserved spot in heaven? The whole Goddamned thing sometimes looks like nothing more than a gigantic monstrous hoax!

Today I got to meet Dr. Mankowitz.

He'd stepped on a needle rake in his garden and sustained three deep puncture wounds. This is a hell of a thing because it happened in the middle of a compost heap, organic fertilizer, etc. We shot him full of T.A.T., anti-Welch bacillus, and the special soup used against all gas anaerobic bacilli, plus penicillin. Then we called Morgan, who came in and didn't like what he heard and saw at all. He felt that Mankowitz should be taken to the O.R. and that the wounds had to be thoroughly excised—absolutely cleaned out. Of course, this requires general anesthesia and comes under the heading of major surgery. Seems like a lot for an awful little, but Morgan told us that the procedure is absolutely indicated considering the depth of the wounds and the geography in which they were received. This, even though the punctures seem trivial. He has complete function of his foot, with no nerve, muscle, or vessel involvement. Morgan says the chance of gas-bacillus infection is maybe one in twenty, which are fairly frightening odds because this one is a killer. Mankowitz saw the logic, was apprehensive and annoyed but agreeable, and up he went. He seems like a nice guy—maybe I'll get to talk to him a bit in the couple of days he's our guest.

L.U.P. and Sailor are status quo. The air conditioner helps a bit but not enough to really matter. His mother is beginning to look pretty worn out.

Today they had a big internist-diagnostician type in on consult from Cedars to see L.U.P. He said to continue the electrolyte route.

Mankowitz is fine and went home today, but we spent an hour in his room talking before he left. This guy is O.K., really very nice. He's Jewish and went to a foreign school, so maybe I'm so prejudiced in his behalf that he can do no wrong. He's an attending here and at the V.A. and has been out of his residency fifteen years. This makes him about forty-five or so. He gets a considerable number of re-

ferrals from the doctors here and gives the staff attendings a
lecture about every three months, which he says is surprisingly well attended. He clued me in to a number of things.
He's been in analysis and had some analytic training, but
he didn't complete it and is not a graduate of an analytic
institute. He says the residency training program at the
V.A. is excellent (I still haven't heard—hope I get in). He
spent two years there and one year at L.A. County. He
feels that personal analysis, while not required unless you
are in formal training in an analytic institute, is an absolute necessity. He said if he had to do it over again he
would become an analyst. You can enter an institute after
two years of residency training, concurrent with the third
year of residency. Analytic institute training usually takes
about four years but can take longer. I mentioned my being impressed with Karen Horney. He told me that he was,
too, and that Horney broke with the Freudians ten years
back. However, there is only one Horney institute and it's
in New York. There are two Freudian institutes in L.A.
One of them is less orthodox and not too unlike Horney in
its approach. Anyway, he feels that analytic training is
extremely important because psychoanalysis is the real basis
for therapy conducted with private neurotic patients. We
spoke about the foreign grad thing (Mankowitz says the
foreign med school never hampered him an iota), which
led to the Jewish bit. Now, here's a discovery: he says that
there are two medical camps in this country, there is Jewish
medicine and there is Gentile medicine. This applies to
hospitals, societies, and feelings in general. Patients cross
lines, and there is a little overlapping here and there, but
not a hell of a lot. He gave himself as an example of over-

lapping. Interns don't count as much as the others, though there are often pretty fixed divisions among interns, too, in large prestigious institutions. There's less of this in psychiatry, but there are mostly Jews in psychiatry, and psychiatry is pretty well divorced from the main body of medicine. He feels that people in other specialties are suspicious of psychiatrists and particularly of analysts. G.P.s tend for the most part to refer to "shockiatrists." These are guys who mainly use electro-shock therapy—often whether it's indicated or not. The only indications for E.C.T. as far as Mankowitz is concerned are catotonic reactions and very deep depressions. He says that he recently saw a paranoid schizophrenic who received twenty E.C.T.s. The man started out well-oriented, well-functioning but delusional. E.C.T. left him poorly oriented, unable to function, and still delusional (he thought the F.B.I. was trying to poison him). Unfortunately, G.P.s prefer any modality that is related to a physiological approach and distrust "unscientific treatment" like "talk sessions." He told me that California itself is a very strange state and that this applies to patients as well as to medicine. Two extremes are found here: ultra sophistication and extreme primitiveness "bordering on aboriginal magic." He points out that all kinds of people come here from all over the country hoping to solve their problems and to start new lives. Since this doesn't happen (they bring themselves and their problems with them), there is much psychiatric business as well as many suicide attempts. He said that there are a great many people here from the Bible belt who are the ready victims of all kinds of quack faith healers and out-and-out charlatans of every variety as well as the "all-American ultra-right-wing conservative politicians" who are fascists at heart. Amazing how little of this I've encountered, but I guess not so amazing considering how sheltered I've been. I've hardly left this place this whole year.

I told him about my medicine/psychiatry conflict, which he said is perfectly rational. He claims that medical training develops a sense of responsibility for patients and an ability to make decisions which are simply not found in any other discipline. Also: that he has picked up physiological dyscrasias in psychiatric patients a number of times in his practice. Also: that it makes it much easier on a patient if his therapist can communicate medically with other specialists should the need arise.

All this made me feel considerably better, and it felt good just to talk to this guy, who is very nice and who is a psychiatrist, which is what I want to be.

I'll feel better yet if and when I'm accepted at the V.A. I hope it wasn't a mistake to apply to just one place. But I understand I can get into a state hospital program at the last minute if I have to. God forbid—because state hospital work is short on training and is mostly custodial functioning, with little or no teaching—just cheap labor.

We had a hell of a scare today! A young kid came in with every clinical evidence of mengio meningitis—stiff neck, high temp, neuro findings, the works. He was transferred to the county hospital's infectious division, which apparently is the routine in these cases. Meanwhile, every inch of the E.R. had to be scrubbed and disinfected and then we had to get rid of our clothes from the skin out and shower and scrub. All we need is an epidemic of meningitis around here, but it's not likely—I hope.

A thirty-five-year-old woman came in this afternoon (after we were all disinfected) and said that she'd been hit in the breast accidentally by her twelve-year-old son. She was afraid that this might cause cancer and she thought she already had a "lump." She said that what made her particularly afraid was the fact that she had no pain, and she had heard a painless lump was a sure sign of malignancy. Morgan was there and he reassured her that cancer does not start from trauma in this way and never starts from anything at all in a matter of several hours. He was, I must say, extremely patient and gentle with her. She still seemed apprehensive, and he offered to examine her, which he did, and he again reassured her, adding that there was absolutely no lump of any kind. She seemed to feel better, and then he slowly and as easy as you please got her to tell him that her mother (still alive) had a radical mastectomy ten years ago and that she has been terrified of breast C.A. ever since. After she left, Morgan told us about C.A. and cardiac phobias. He pointed out that telling patients too much can kick off phobic reactions that can last a lifetime, but that telling them too little can be very frustrating to them and make them feel that M.D.s are arrogant, etc.—it's a case of damned if you do, damned if you don't. This kicked off a discussion about telling or not telling patients about terminal disease. Morgan feels this is a highly individual decision and must be evaluated in terms of the patient's particular psychology, as well as the kind of relatives he has (is there someone responsible who can be told?) and his status in life generally. "All in all, it's a bitch of a decision, and a Goddamned important one!" I brought up the whole issue of mastectomy and especially radical mastectomy. I had heard the argument that by the time a lesion is detectable surgery is pointless, because metastasis is already present. Also, that statistically people do about the same longevity-wise with and without surgery. I also read that in England findings are that simple mastectomy is just as effective as radical. Morgan says that the anti-surgical argument is once again an example of "statistical bullshit" as well as medical nihilism. He says simple versus radical may well be true and that surgeons in the U.S. are probably inclined to radicals so as to avoid lawsuits, which are not as prevalent in England. No one can accuse a doctor of not having done his utmost if he removes all the nodes and lymphatics as well as the breast. He admitted, though, that a radical is one hell of a maiming procedure. He'd read an article recently in which it is suggested that three nodes be biopsied: sternal, axillary, and lateral chest. If there are no metastases then a radical is suggested, because there is still time to save the patient. If metastases are found, it is too late to clean out nodes, and surgery should be limited to a simple. I have to admit it: Morgan is really knowledgeable as hell, and rather compassionate and sensitive, too. His treatment of the breast-phobic woman seems to indicate that he is not without psychological know-how, either. I sit here now and I realize that I've already been making comparisons between the two M's, Morgan and Mankowitz. Morgan, the champion of surgery, and Mankowitz, the champion of psychiatry—and I would have liked to find Mank vastly superior. Here I've been bitching about the dichotomy and antipathy that exist between psychiatry and the rest of medicine, and here I am creating exactly the same thing—with representative champions yet. What an oversimplification! Of course,

Morgan is not representative of anything or anybody but himself, and I'm sure the same is true of Mank. From what I've read in Horney, I think that what I'm doing is polarizing issues so as to simplify my conflict. If Morgan is narrow, repressed, constricted, and crass, and Mankowitz is cultured, open, sophisticated, and sensitive, then obviously psychiatry is superior to lowly surgery, and then I can feel that I give up nothing when I leave here. I think Horney calls this streamlining. Anyway, it has nothing to do with reality. Both these guys are O.K., and right now it wouldn't surprise me at all to find out that Mankowitz knows his medicine as well as he does psychiatry. By the way, he graduated from Edinburgh (not quite as foreign as Lausanne), and as I said he never found it a hindrance. Not a single patient or anybody else since he started to practice has asked to look at his diplomas and credentials.

I visited "my" patients upstairs twice today. L.U.P. shows no change at all. Mrs. James is sitting up reading, knitting, and seemingly very comfortable. She's one of the few—I think the only—real native-born Californian I've met. Her people came here prior to the Gold-Rush days. She's really quite a gal. Sailor's condition remains unchanged, but his legs look and smell terrible.

I had a sensational ego boost today. Morgan brought a new guy in, a forty-to-forty-five-year-old Hungarian doctor by the name of Lazo. This brings us up to four regulars on E.R. Lazo is not an intern or resident—he's through with all that. He simply has a regular job working in the E.R. I wonder what they pay him. I watched him all day, and he seems to know his stuff. He's a big husky guy but moves very quickly—and quietly. He hardly said a word except for a few questions he asked me. I thought maybe he was shy because of language difficulty, but though he has a heavy accent his English is pretty good. The boost: Morgan tells him and everyone else who is there to hear that if any question comes up and Morgan or Madden can't be reached, to ask me—Rubin is in charge. Just like that—I heard it in so many words! Even now as I write this, I think of the $1,000 and I feel the joy of Morgan's confidence in me melting away. But the hell with it—I've got to admit I respect Morgan and therefore find it particularly gratifying that he respects me. I guess it also mitigates the second-class citizen thing a bit too. I've got to get over that number once and for all. I suppose I have plenty of what Horney calls "neurotic pride."

Today something happened that was funny as hell, and it also shows how rigidified and stupid you can get by thoughtlessly using routine procedures and neglecting the obvious or common sense.

We had a room full of people, a load of patients, four of us, two nurses' aides and Logan's stand-in, Betty Smith, a very nice girl but only half as fast as the Log. Anyway, two of us, Lazo and me, were desperately trying to get a marble out of a four-year-old girl's nose with all kinds of probes and forceps, while Roger was packing a sixty-nine-year-old woman's nose with adrenalin. She was bleeding furiously. Anterior packs hadn't worked, and he was now on to posterior packs.

Aiken, the E.N.T. man, suddenly materialized out of nowhere. Said he was just walking through on his way upstairs. (This place somehow attracts everyone like flypaper. I think it's mostly curiosity, finding the unexpected. Maybe also it's the frenetic pace of everything here that stimulates feelings of aliveness. Funny that here in the middle of so many kinds of human troubles and death itself there is this kind of alive thing generated, but it's so. The O.R. had the same quality, but not nearly as much intensity. Sounds melodramatic as hell, but I suppose given an area where everyone is working to save life, you're bound to have a sense of your own aliveness generated.) Anyway, Aiken goes over to Roger, removes all the adrenalin packs, and tells Rog to just pinch the patient's nose, the entire soft section, for about ten minutes, real firmly. He says that 90 percent of nosebleeds occur in Heserlblach's triangle, the soft tissue area, and that pinching will almost always cause clotting. He then walks over to our case, gently takes forceps and nasal speculum out of our hands, and closes the kid's free nostril with his index finger and shouts, "Blow!" The kid blows and out comes the marble. Ten minutes later he tells Rog to stop pinching, and the woman's nosebleed has stopped. We kept her another half hour after Aiken left; the nosebleed didn't recur and we sent her home. This is a clear-cut case of federalizing the simple! Frankly though, we were so Goddamned busy and so tired we didn't have either the time or the energy to be embarrassed. I've learned a lesson though, several in fact: Use common sense! Don't complicate matters with fancy procedures! Keep an open mind! Keep loose, flexible! All this sounds so easy, but I suppose it becomes that much harder when you're under the gun, busy and tired. But I've definitely learned how to stop nosebleeds and how to get marbles out of noses!

There were a bunch of consultations down here today on Sailor. They're afraid of his losing his legs. Apparently there's been a change in temperature and color, and it seems that his lower limb circulation is getting loused up by all this bone exposure, injury and infection. Anyway, the big news is that they're going to operate! Of course, all this open reduction work is going to take place upstairs in the O.R., and then they will keep him upstairs on surgery. The navy is sending a Dr. Richard Stonehouse, who is being given courtesy privileges to operate by our hospital. He's supposed to be one of the best orthopods in the country. I was wondering whether or not they will anesthetize Sailor, inasmuch as he doesn't respond to pain or anything else anyway.

They moved Sailor today, and I went up to see him. Seems unfamiliar and strange not having him next door. He's exactly the same as before, and apparently no worse for the move. They probably could have done this when he first came in—but who knows? Anyway, second-guessing is a hell of a destructive enterprise, especially in medicine. I hope he comes through surgery O.K. and God willing this guy Stonehouse will save his legs. Anyway, they operate tomorrow A.M.

Mrs. James is dead. Just like that. She died last night. On the way to see Sailor I stopped by her room, and it was empty. Johnson told me they found her dead during the night, that there was no time for any treatment, nothing at all. She was all alone. She had the best treatment, including anticoagulants, sedation for anxiety, etc., and none of it helped. It must have been a massive coronary. Johnson was right. I feel terrible. I started to cry while I was speaking to him; I hope he didn't notice. I don't think I could get used to this business. I just don't have Johnson's kind of detachment. Maybe I am a hell of a lot better off in psychiatry. I just spoke to her and she seemed so cheerful, and now, just like that—she's gone.

Sailor seemed exactly the same, none the worse for his operation. I hope his legs mend O.K. Morgan first-assisted and says Stonehouse did a beautiful job. The major concern is circulation. They can't anticoagulate him for fear of stirring up intracranial bleeding, because sure as hell something no good is going on in his brain. They gave him light anesthesia and he didn't stir an iota.

Last night I dreamed something about women and how they are not supposed to die of coronaries.

Just can't get over the fact that Mrs. James is dead. I guess I convinced myself that she was going to make it. With minimal anastomosis around the heart, people under fifty have so much less chance of making it than older people with infarcts.

Sailor's legs are warm! Please God, he shouldn't blow an embolus or anything crazy!

Was thinking about life and death and the whole lousy bit. Mrs. James again. Had a muddled dream about her that I can't remember. Hope L.U.P. and Sailor make it. In my dream there was something about Madden's pulmonary embolus case, too. I guess psychiatrists can have pretty rough times, too, deciding whether or not a guy is dangerous or suicidal and should or shouldn't be hospitalized. I suppose I'm just feeling tired and morbid. It's not all fun and games, and the good guys don't always win.

Sailor's legs look fine. I think they're going to be O.K. After Mrs. James, I'm afraid to say, but Morgan agrees. I hope we are right! Jesus, is that what I've been having, a pride reaction, because I called it wrong on Mrs. James? Maybe; I've been feeling sort of depressed. All work, no play? I do feel bad about her—a very nice person who is now gone—but that feeling and my having a pride reaction are not mutually exclusive. Could use a lift—where is the answer from the V.A., the bastards? Is it possible that I'm afraid? Doctors get infarcts, too.

Speaking of depression, an eighteen-year-old boy came in today who was so depressed he could hardly move. I think this is called "psychomotor retardation." He made a half-hearted attempt to cut his wrists. I managed to get him into a conversation of sorts. He was able to speak only in one-word answers in an extremely low, slow voice. What he had to say was that he was not doing well in school and that he knew his parents would be terribly disappointed in him. Seems so strange that someone could develop this kind of awful sense of proportion about the relative importance of things and issues. I was working up a big head of hate for his parents when they came in. They seemed nice enough and terribly concerned. His father was quite distraught. They said that the boy had always been perfectionistic and that he was doing O.K. in school but not up to his own standards. They had felt that he needed psychiatric care for some time. I mentioned Dr. Mankowitz (my first psychiatric referral), and they jotted down his name. Who knows whether the kid will go or not. So many people leave here, and of course we have no idea of whatever happens to them.

I guess this boy pretty well demonstrated Horney's self-hate business and the self-glorification thing. Terrible, the standards we make for ourselves and the punishment we deal out when we don't meet them. This kid had the furtive look of a criminal, and in terms of his awful conscience I guess that's how he feels.

Seems funny, Sailor being upstairs and no longer being "our case." The side room still feels strange and empty without him. Crazy thing is I spoke to Rog and Kurt, and it turns out all three of us (Lazo the Silent One doesn't know him) have been going up at least once a day to see him. I guess we feel he is still our case. Anyway, he is now under the official care of Alvin Johnson even though he is on the surgical service. They're more thorough than we are down here. They've done blood counts, E.K.G.s, blood chemistries, and a load of things—but not spinal tap, E.E.G., or skull films, since these would jolt him too much. There's been no talk of putting his shoulder together, maybe because it's in fairly good position. Their tests and big fancy management procedures and elaborate chartings haven't produced anything more than we've done downstairs. Writing this, I realize I'm beginning to sound jealous and kind of possessive—a rather peculiar manifestation! Anyway, Sailor seems to be doing O.K. Speak of sense of proportion and relativity—I mean he's O.K. in the legs department, but I wonder if there's any chance at all that he will ever get to use them.

Got the Goddamned thing! Got the letter! I've been accepted! They wanted an immediate reply, and I sent it— I accept! I accept! I'll be there July 1 for sure. I guess I still feel surprised when I'm wanted—still traumatized by the whole medical school bit. The minus-$1,000, second-class feeling doesn't help either. Will I ever let go of this crap? Anyway, now that I've got it, it already seems anticlimactic. Besides, the V.A. and the whole psychiatric thing are still a million E.R. light years away.

Alvin Johnson has called Mankowitz in on L.U.P.! I guess they've run out of ideas. I heard her family is applying a hell of a lot of pressure. Incidentally, her baby is just fine. For the hell of it, I checked into it today and there was no Rh business or anything like that. I've got to manage to be there tomorrow when Mank sees her.

Alvin Johnson, Mank, L.U.P., and her special and of course me—we were the only ones there. Mank just stepped into her doorway and whispered a diagnosis: "Catatonic reaction." Just like that, he said he knew that's what it was. He then went over and bent her arms this way and that and told us that he was fairly sure that this was a postpartum, acute catatonic reaction even though there was no waxy flexibility. He said he thought that he could bring her out then and there with Amital, but that she would go back into the stupor again when the Amital wore off. He said the treatment of choice was E.C.T., and that if this was a solitary acute reaction, this might bring her out and that she might sustain consciousness, in which case she could go home with a nurse and see a psychiatrist on the outside. He told Johnson to get her husband to stop by his office to sign the necessary forms and that he would shock her tomorrow A.M. What can I say? Both of us, Johnson and I, were deeply shocked. Nobody ever mentioned this possibility at all as part of a differential diagnosis. I was more than shocked; I realize that I immediately identified with Mank, who I thought was being unduly certain, cocky, and even arrogant. I mean, how can he be so sure? What if she doesn't respond? We'll both look like awful fools. I don't know what possessed me, because not only did I tell everyone in the E.R. the new diagnosis, I also told them I was sure Mank was right. Why? I'm not sure at all. The fact is, she doesn't at all remind me of the couple of catatonics I saw in my psych class, but they weren't acute and they weren't postpartum.

What can I write here? Mank came off like the eighth wonder of the world! This was magic, miracle, Jesus Christ and omnipotence all wrapped in one, and I feel that I somehow came off as the recipient of most of this glory and prestige, because I am the only one in this joint going into psychiatry. To make matters best, everyone was there —I mean everyone from our place that has had anything at all to do with L.U.P. The word must have really gotten around, because there were at least twenty people jamming the room. I'm sure some of them came to see us fail—us, mind you!—but no one said a word, and Mank couldn't have been cooler. He had this portable E.C.T. machine with him that he plugged into the wall, turned a few dials, put a headband and two round discs smeared with salty KY jelly on her forehead, had two of us hold her ankles and shoulders, and he pressed the button. Her body came up against our hands, she took a long deep breath, turned blue, and went into a grand mal seizure—all in all a terrible sight. She convulsed for what seemed like hours, but I guess it was only for several seconds. The guttural sound from her throat was awful. (I forgot to say that her teeth were clamped down on the mouthpiece we had in-serted.) Her face got darker and darker, and I wondered if she'd ever breathe again. I could see Mank and me drawn and quartered right in the room. If there is such a thing as acute Jewish paranoia, I was having an attack then and there. But, after forever, she finally let the air out, took a deep breath and got rosy-colored again. The twitching stopped and her body relaxed. I swear there was a sigh of relief in unison in that damned room. Mank re-moved the head band and electrode discs and washed her face with a wet compress. After a few minutes she began to talk. What she said wasn't really intelligible. She seemed very sleepy and made a jumble of words, but she spoke.

No question about it, she was conscious, maybe not fully, but on a level that was a thousand times more alive than she had been for days. Of course, I thought of Sailor, but E.C.T. would kill anyone who had sustained a head injury. Everyone was really astounded. There was no doubt at all about the diagnosis. Each and every one went over and shook hands with Mank, who seemed somewhat embarrassed. When I shook his hand, he said that anyone would have made the diagnosis if she had been on a psychiatric ward. Since she was on internal medicine following a simple delivery in a general hospital, everyone was thrown off. Geography then made the difference; and also, I suppose, everyone tends to confine his thinking to his own specialty (Horney's neurotic pride?). I've got to remember to try to keep an open head in psychiatric matters in the future. But I still think that Mank was being unduly modest. Insane thing is that several people patted me on the back, too. Rog and Morgan actually shook my hand. That's identification for you. Not only that, I felt that it was somehow appropriate—me getting congratulated, too. I guess psychiatry, Jews, Mank and I and foreign schools, we're all vindicated when he pushed the button on that little gadget this A.M. Truth is, at one point I felt like saying, "Now, don't you all feel sorry—shove the $1,000 up your asses a dollar at a time." Well I hope they don't hate us later when they calm down, in a sort of delayed hurt-pride reaction. But I couldn't care less. I guess I'd trade being liked for admiration. Anyway, enough of my acute paranoia and my pilot-fishing myself to Mank's glory. Before he left he said he would shock her again this evening and tomorrow morning, and then would see how it goes. I guess Johnson deserves credit for calling in Mank, but it's hard to recognize that in view of all his electrolyte crap. Christ, I've just got to learn to be less critical. Fact is, the possibility of a psychiatric reaction never occurred to me at all. But there I go again with exhorbitant demands on myself. Why should it occur to me? I have had no experience at all with this kind of thing other than this one.

I couldn't get away to see any more of it, but I heard that L.U.P.'s response was fantastic! She's out of it—a bit hazy, but out. She's being discharged this evening and Mank will be her doctor on the outside. How fast glory passes, because all this already seems anticlimactic. What does linger on though is the feeling that—see! I'm absolutely right to have chosen psychiatry! Of course this is really insane, because I'm obviously as prejudiced about psychiatry as the other guys. Why else would I be so impressed by the facts that 1. psychiatric clinical syndromes exist; 2. there are people who are trained to recognize them; and 3. successful treatment is possible?

We had seven—*seven*—cases today of metal corneal implants. I spudded three of them out and the Silent One (Lazo) did the others. I curetted the abrasions as much as possible, but I know sure as hell there's bound to be some rust ring. Get overzealous in a thing like this and you can do more harm than good. On the other hand, get too timid and you can get some kind of permanent corneal rust tattoo and foreign-body reaction, all of which doesn't exactly improve the vision. I console myself with the fact that these guys will all be followed up by their ophthalmologists—I hope! Actually, I *know* they will—because tomorrow when that procaine solution wears off, they're going to hurt like hell, even with the pressure patch we applied. Having had a simple corneal abrasion myself, I know how much pain these can make. In this case, the pain's good, because it will guarantee a proper follow-up—me and my damnable, overworking, overtime superego.

We had a woman in today who didn't make it. A carbon-monoxide garage case, an obvious suicide. We sent her upstairs and they transfused whole blood, almost completely exchanging her entire blood supply, but it didn't work; also adrenalin, cortisone, Coramine—all no dice. I wonder if she had hoped to be found in time. She couldn't have been more than thirty, and rather pretty. Morgan says the pretty look is largely from the carbon monoxide, which links with hemoglobin twice as fast as oxygen, loading the blood with carboxyhemoglobin in lieu of oxyhemoglobin. Since this linkage is more fixed than that of the O_2 linkage, once they have that carboxy cherry look chances are there's damn little hemoglobin left in the red cells to pick up O_2 in the lungs. So these people literally choke to death internally. Theoretically massive exchange of this monoxide-loaded blood for oxygenated blood should help, but Morgan says it doesn't. By the way, he told me why we are getting all the eye cases: several new factories making airplane parts have opened around here and they are employing lathe workers who are too green to know to keep their goggles on while working around metals. They should really have a full-time eye man on duty all the time; otherwise we will be the overworked victims of their carelessness.

A young doctor (only thirty-two) came in today D.O.A., and it really shook us all up. Nobody knew him. He lived near here but worked elsewhere. I suppose his being a doctor got to us. The hangman also dies! I guess we're crazy enough to believe that we are a species apart and have some special protection or something. But this got to us for another, stronger reason: this guy was a suicide, a very grotesque suicide. They found him dead in his bathroom. He lived alone and worked in a blood bank or something out in the valley. He had a towel around his neck, and when they removed it they saw how he died. He had performed very neat surgery on himself—skin retracted, vessels tied off, all very neat and skillful—right down to the jugulars, both of which were hemisected and dangling. There were surgical instruments, procaine and syringe (he had anesthetized himself) and blood all over the place. Roger looked at his neck when he came in, but I didn't. Why should I subject myself to what I know would bother the daylights out of me? From the little I know of the suicidal types, this man sounds schizophrenic. I guess doctors can be psychotic, too.

Speaking of schizophrenia, I sat with Mank in the dining room today. L.U.P., who is now a real person called Mrs. Martin, twenty-eight years old, is doing O.K., or at least as O.K. as she did prior to her delivery and acute reaction. She had five E.C.T.s and no more are necessary. Her memory is a little cloudy but Mank says that will return; otherwise she's O.K. He says that she is a very dependent, inadequate, immature kind of person and probably has had mild undetected episodes in the past. She's always been a rather withdrawn schizoid type, he thinks. He feels that she functions O.K. on a limited and protected basis, and real digging would probably reveal an underlying psychotic process (this I don't really understand and was too self-effacing to ask about, since I'm also grandiose enough to already feel like we're colleagues). He told me that she's very poorly motivated and is a lousy candidate for psychotherapy, so he will probably not see her again after a few weeks. He plans to tell her husband and herself that it would be best to stop at two kids, though he doesn't think she really needs this warning. Interestingly, most postpartum reactions are psychotic depressions, but he's seen a number of catatonics and hebephrenics, too. He says that all three often overlap, and this may well be the case with Mrs. Martin. Also, as with her, most of them occur after the second delivery. Why? No one knows. Some people think there's an unconscious dynamic reason of some kind, a reminder of one's own sibling rivalry or some other such theory. Some psychiatrists believe that it's purely on an organic basis, hormonal or allergic or something. No one really knows. We also spoke about doctors in general—gossip, I guess. He said that if more G.P.s took the time to speak to their patients, fewer psychiatrists would be necessary. I told him that I was accepted at the V.A. program. He assured me of its excellence as a training program and welcomed me to the "club," which really felt nice. I like this guy. He's straightforward and completely lacking in any kind of fancy pretense.

I caught Sailor's mother in tears today—what I mean is that I came into Sailor's room and there she was, quietly sobbing, trying to muffle it all in a handkerchief. When she saw me, she became terribly embarrassed, as if she had committed a crime or something. This made me feel quite embarrassed, too, because I knew I had burst in on a very private scene. I felt like going over and putting my arms around her and hugging and comforting her, and instead I made with some stupid words that I don't remember, felt extremely stiff and awkward, and left as soon as I could. Why can't people allow themselves to feel, let alone show and share their feelings? Why are we so Goddamned cruel and austere with ourselves? There's surely something radically wrong with a world that makes us so inhibited. God, what that poor woman must be going through, and she hasn't permitted herself the luxury of even a little bitching or open weeping or anything. And me? I couldn't permit myself the human urge to go over and pat her on the head or the equivalent. God forbid two people should touch— emotionally touch—and comfort each other in the face of common grief, or, for that matter, at any time they are so moved. Jesus, the insane inner craziness that ties us up— can we ever get rid of it? This having to act so bloody cool, dignified—all this is pure pretense. All of it isn't worth an iota of spontaneously being whatever one is. But how do you recapture that spontaneous thing? It feels like taking a big chance or something. That's how it felt with Sailor's mother. Maybe psychoanalysis helps.

Speaking of pretenses, the funniest thing happened when I left the E.R. tonight. A guy was polishing his old antique Lincoln in the street perpendicular to the ambulance alley. Smithson, me, and Roger got into a conversation with him. This guy is about forty years old. Smithson and me were both dressed in regular clothes and Rog was still in his whites. Well, Smithson and I occasionally use words like hell, damn, and Smithson may even have said fuck or bastard or something. This guy, who is doing his car, suddenly stands up and proceeds to give Smithson and me a long harangue, a real sermon, mind you, on how it's O.K. to talk that way "among ourselves," and he includes himself. But to talk that way in front of a *doctor*—and he points to Rog—is "disrespectful," "very bad," "uncivilized" (he went on and on like this) and "should not be done." Smithson and I felt so put down, talking like this to Rog in front of a civilian, that we went off to have a few beers in the corner gin mill before sacking out.

Let me state here and now that we are involved in a wrestling mania. Yes, in our spare time—of which there is very little—we sit frozen in front of the T.V. set watching wrestling exclusively. Mostly it's Rog, me, and Smithson, but Kurt, too, is gradually getting sucked in, and I've even caught the Silent One sitting and staring at these guys throwing each other around. Of course, we all know that it's phony, all show and no contest, but we've taken a solemn oath to never speak of this. We simply watch, and each of us has his identifying champions. Smithson's are the freaks—Gorgeous George and other eccentrics and villains. Roger's are the athletes, the clean-cut boys. Mine are the Mexicans. Since I've wrestled a bit in college, I know that what I am watching has nothing at all to do with the competitive sport called wrestling, but this doesn't dilute my enthusiasm a bit. We yell, we root, we complain, we pound the seats. Here, watching T.V. wrestling, we can somehow allow ourselves to be uninhibited, free, as crazy as we like—and we like it just fine. I hope this guy Rivera and his brother beat the hell out of these two hillbillies tonight in the tag-team match.

Rivera won!

This Furacin for burns, it's just plain ridiculous. Morgan agrees with me but can see no harm in it. Of course, we were all told in medical school that Rule #1 is to do no harm—but simply doing no harm is a hell of a way to spend one's time. I suppose this Furacin thing gets to me because I hate the damn burns so. Truth is, I never even think of Furacin in connection with suturing, and yet we dress every suture with Furacin. Today we had a four-year-old little girl, badly burned by boiling water off a stove—she'd reached up and pulled it down on herself. It was terrible to hear this baby cry; I just hope to hell she'll be all right. Sometimes I get awfully sick of this lousy place. Seems like we're always in the middle of some kind of insane house of horrors. This is how a battlefield must feel.

A carpenter, fifty-five years old, a tall thin guy, hell of a good humor (though why I don't know), came in with a miserable compound fracture. Amazing—and I'll never understand about the pain thing—he seemed fairly comfortable and, as I said, good-humored. He's one of these simple, nice, earthy people. Why can some people tolerate pain, or don't they feel it as much? Is the threshold for pain an inborn physiological thing, or is it something learned in the way we are brought up? Anyway, speaking of earthy, I'm afraid earth will be his undoing—at least that's what Morgan and Madden say. He fell off this pretty high ladder and fractured his left tibia and fibula, and about four inches of the proximal ends went right through the skin and into the ground. He actually came in here with two big shafts of bone sticking out of his mid-leg still covered with soil. Of course, I thought of Sailor, but Morgan pointed out that Sailor had no soil contamination on his exposed bone, and that his sailor pants (tough cloth, thank the navy) covered the exposed bone. I also thought of Mank and his puncture wounds. Now, that's the thing—the soil! This was rich organically fertilized garden soil, and it had to be loaded with every organism in the book! Of course, we shot him with everything we have, including especially heavy doses of the antitet, Welch, and gas stuff. Then we sent him upstairs, where Madden will clean him up and try to put him together. Morgan says he'll develop an osteo for sure and will probably run pus clean out to the surface for ages to come. Much will depend on his circulation. Morgan thinks he may walk. But even if he walks, he may lose the leg anyway, not from the injury but from the infection. This is one hell of a sequence!

We had kind of a "different" one today. A very pretty thirty-year-old single woman came in who didn't know whether or not she had been raped. This is what happened: She had been asleep when a young guy came in through the window and ransacked her apartment. She woke up and recognized him as a neighbor's son. That's all she remembered, because he must have hit her on the head. She said that when she woke up she "felt funny down there" and didn't know whether he'd added rape to his burglary. There she was in the E.R. with a boyfriend, a room full of cops, a newspaper reporter, and a lawyer. I was beginning to think the whole thing was a publicity hoax of some kind. This is, after all, a pretty crazy show-bizzy town. Anyway, Morgan had her sign some special forms and had them witnessed and cosigned by everyone in the E.R., including her lawyer and one of the cops. We then took her into Sailor's side room (as it will always be known from now on) spread her legs, and did a vaginal smear. She seemed perfectly at ease throughout all this, which made me suspicious, but of what I don't exactly know. She was one hell of a looker, though. We both wondered to what extent she may have unconsciously contributed to the "rape." This is a hell of a thing, being suspicious of the victim—it's like blaming the Jews for getting killed by the Germans. She did have a non-lacerated hematoma the size of a walnut on her scalp; but had she enticed the guy before all this? Who knows? Anyway, I asked her the guy's age, and she said sixteen or seventeen—so again, who knows? When we looked under the scope, the slide was full of sperm, but of course all this is still circumstantial—it could be anyone's sperm. They have not picked up the kid as yet but are apparently out looking for him. In any case, she left with her boyfriend and lawyer and for us that was the end of the story. It just seems funny now, when I think of Morgan looking up this woman's crotch—beautiful legs, beautiful the whole works—and unfortunately (this does not make me proud) his cool detachment made her seem like a lab animal of some kind. Fact is, I spoke to her during the "procedure," but Morgan never said a word.

I now have a big reputation in this institution, developed over this whole year, as a veno-puncture artist. I really have. I've developed the feel and knack of finding a usable vein—that is, if one exists at all in the case in question. This doesn't seem like much of a talent, but since everyone hates to do cut-downs, it is much appreciated around these parts. Anyway, I'm batting about .900 and consequently feel that my rep is at stake every time I have a tough one. I must admit, patting myself on the back, that I tried to teach Rog and Kurt and even the Silent One the technique, and they do O.K. but not as good as the old maître. It was actually the old maître of polyclinic surgery in Lausanne who taught me the trick, that feeling the vein is more important than seeing it. If you can feel it with your fingertips (and mine seem to be pretty adept at this), then all you have to do is slap it a few times to bring it up, fix it with your thumb so it doesn't roll, and stick it. It almost always works. So, today I had the challenge of challenges. They called me upstairs to do an I.V. on a post-op guy (diaphragmatic hernia repair) rapidly going into shock. But this guy weighed about 400 pounds. He had a layer of fat a mile thick covering everything. Several people working the floors, from both medicine and surgery, had tried to pop him, and all he had to show for it were a bunch of black-and-blue marks. He was in a hell of a cold sweat and getting quite shocky looking, so I could see that a cut-down ought to be done in the next several minutes. If the blood pressure in a fellow this weight goes down, it may never come up again. The duty nurse knew this, too, because she had the cut-down set already prepared and the first-year surgical resident was on his way over from staff to do it. If all this sounds dramatic, it's because it was. So I tied my tourniquet and all I saw was fat, and I felt with my fingers and there was still more fat—all very sweaty and slippery. I dried him off, felt around, and I hit something. There was the faintest semblance of a fine ridge just lateral to the left cubital fossa. I hit it, fixed it, had the nurse stand by with the I.V. set, and stuck him and struck oil. The nurse couldn't stop praising me—actually called me "a genius." I blushed but lapped up every word of it and was a big hero when I got back downstairs again, because she'd telephoned my victory in advance of my arrival. Any more ego-gratification and I'll surely burst with the fullness of my self-importance. Now, the question is: is the feeling that this kind of thing gives me (à la K. Horney) neurotic pride? Real self? Or both? If I pooh-poohed it to myself as being "nothing at all," would this be self-hate, duplicity, false modesty, self-effacement, reality—or all of the above? All this will have to wait for my analysis. In the meantime, I must say it feels good to get something going that the other guys couldn't, however simple a thing it may be. Is this a form of sadism or vindictive triumph? Maybe, but screw it—I don't care. I'm tired, and I'm sacking out!

I thought I'd sack out, but here I am writing again, because they got busy as hell and needed me. Among other things, I had a bit of a deflation. Can't win them all! A six-year-old girl came in bleeding like crazy from a post-op tonsillectomy. We tried to get her private M.D., but no dice. So we called Bill Aiken and in the meantime I.V.d her while I tried to stop the blood. Jesus, this thing was so scary that we pumped blood in under pressure, because the way she was losing it I felt she'd be bled out in no time. Of course, the tea-bag routine didn't work at all—hence my deflation (but a very minor one at that). I knew it was an artery, but with her screaming and flailing around I just couldn't see it. We used suction and tried to keep the thing clear, but it was hopeless. For a while she began to gag so on her own blood that I thought we'd better trache her. Aiken finally got there, and this time there was no nose-pinching gimmick. He said these cases were most dangerous and sent her up to the O.R., where they put her under general and tied it off. When he came down he told us she was just fine and that this one was the E.N.T. man's classic nightmare. I guess every specialty has at least one. I remember our surgery professor telling about gastrectomy and nightmares involving blowout of the duodenal stump. I guess in psychiatry it's suicide and murder on the part of psychotic patients. Speaking of suicides, I just thought of the 400-pound fat man I.V.d up there. I've assisted on a few very fat surgical cases—it's like operating in a deep well, and they're always prone to shock. This guy is thirty-five and is sure as shit an excellent candidate for a C.V.A. or coronary. But who am I to talk—I'm up to 250 again, and this, too, is surely self-destructive as hell and I don't need analysis to know that. I got to get my ass into the dieting sling as of this A.M. for sure and STAT!

Tonight on T.V. I saw this guy Two-Ton Tommy wrestling. He looked just like the post-op guy upstairs. Of course, since he's a freak, Smithson roots for him. How does a guy like this keep from croaking? I just don't understand it! I guess I'm feeling particularly virtuous because I dieted all day. Hope I can fall asleep, because I'm hungry as hell.

Here I am in the middle of C.V.A.s, heart failures, coronaries, and I still eat like a pig! Why? Because I'm always tired. The hours we work are inhuman. People just aren't meant to work twenty-four on, or even twelve on, and then be on call if it gets busy, which inevitably means a chopped-up sleepless night. I guess I have the peculiar misbegotten emotional idea (emotional because I don't believe it with logic in my head) that food makes energy that keeps me up and going. I think that it's actually more likely that the process of eating—the actual chewing, swallowing, etc.—gives me some kind of gratification that makes up for the gratification proper sleep would bring. Who knows? But I do know that internships are ridiculous. The Silent One works ten hours a day, while we work twelve and on call for twenty-four straight through. Does our internship status make us supermen or less vulnerable to fatigue? Frankly, I'm surprised more mistakes aren't made around here, because how can you be maximally efficient if you're going around like the walking dead? The whole thing is, I suspect, a cheap-labor device, and pretty disgusting on the part of the medical profession. People say this makes for toughness and an ability to work under pressure, etc. Maybe so; but it also makes for bitterness and cynicism and may account for exceptionally high fees some M.D.s charge to make up for this kind of unpaid slavery. In my case, though, it also makes for over-weight. Is that what all this bitching is about, my inability to control my eating? I'm up to 257, more than I've ever weighed in my life. Maybe I ought to start smoking. But I can still see the people on the chest ward in Lausanne coughing up blood and cancerous lung tissue. The hell with that! But I am tired, and here's why:

This day was a typical (if there is such a thing) E.R. stint, over twelve hours, manned by three doctors and three nurses, with occasional help from Morgan and other wan-derers from the floors upstairs. The following report comes from the write-ups on the charts, on which my name ap-pears for at least its fair share. I'll do it like a physical, from the head down, because, interestingly enough, there's hardly a bit of human anatomy we missed:

Two barbiturate overdoses: I lavaged one. One went up-stairs, one went home. Both are "saved."

One Antroll kid: Lavaged by Rog.

One psychotic girl: About sixteen, she talked gibberish half the time, echoed anything I said a quarter of the time, and talked in rhymes a quarter of the time. They found her wandering about on Santa Monica Boulevard, dodging cars and trucks. I think they call her kind of verbal out-put a thought-disorder or word-salad and/or echolalia. She seems to fit the textbook description of hebephrenia. She was very childish and sort of "silly." Anyway, no treatment on her. Her parents came for her and were reluctant to give me any background, just that she's sixteen and "has never been quite right but never harmed anyone." (This was my chart. I get the psychiatric ones.)

One old man: A rather sweet guy, also confused and wandering about, who is obviously suffering from senile psychosis. The V.A. came for him and told us he wanders out of the V.A. hospital, where he's lived for years, and gets lost about twice a year. He gave a perfect example of confabulation. He was completely disoriented in time, place, and person, but when I suggested any "fact" to him, he filled in the rest.

Me: "You are a hundred and eight years old?"
Him: "Yes, a hundred and eight."
Me: "Your name is Woodrow Hoover?"
Him: "Woodrow, that's me—a hundred and three years old."
Me: "From New England?"
Him: "London, England—yes."

Et cetera. Another psychiatric Rubin-signed special!

Two nosebleeds: One was an elderly woman with high blood pressure—210/110. Pinching didn't do it. I packed her with adrenalin. She went upstairs under care of one of the attending internists whom I don't know. The other was a kid—Rog pinched the nose with 100 percent success.

Wait now—I'm out of my top-down order: the head comes before the nose.

Two possible skull fractures: Normal pupillary responses, no blood out of ears, and no history of unconsciousness. Skull plates were neg, and both went home to be treated by their own M.D.s.

Seven scalp lacerations: Four kids, three adults (three sutured by me); all sent home.

One woman with a history of glaucoma: She was afraid that she was going blind—and I mean *now!* This turned out to be hysterical reaction. I signed the chart, and she will see her M.D. in the A.M.

Three simple eye foreign bodies: None treated by me.

Two corneal implants: Metal chips (a slow night), neither curetted out by me.

One bug in a kid's ear: Removed by me. Believe it or not, I hardly remember this one, but I signed the chart.

A woman came in to have her ears pierced and was outraged when we turned her down.

Two otitis media: One kid and one adult. I treated both with hot oil and penicillin and referred to rotating E.N.T. attendings off list.

One toothache: Filled with oil of cloves by Rog.

Three eyebrow lacerations: One girl was sutured by Kurt, who nearly had her eyebrow shaved off; others by me.

Two closed-eye hematomas: One man, and one woman hit by husband. Black eyes, no complications, though I wonder why these blows on eyes don't do vast damage. Bony orbit obviously affords much protection.

Two lip lacerations: I got one.

Two sore throats: Sent them home to their own M.D.s.

One diaper-pin swallower: Had this kid X-rayed—pin is closed and will come out in the wash.

One severe migraine: Gave Emp and codeine #4 and sent home.

One dizziness: No elevated B.P. and no findings; maybe too much sun. Sent home to own M.D.

One D.O.A. drowning: A forty-seven-year-old man. For all the swimming that goes on here, there are surprisingly few drownings. Most Californians swim from birth, but most Californians are not Californians, and we get one now and then.

One acute gall bladder: With history of similar attacks. Could be a faking addict, but gave Demerol and referred her to own M.D. Belly was soft, no acute abdomen.

I'm skipping again—back to the upper regions.

One woman with a fish bone in pharynx: Removed by Rog.

One woman who couldn't swallow: Seemed hysterical —globus hystericus? Reassured her and gave her some Luminal; sent her to Aiken, the next E.N.T. man off list.

Two C.V.A.s: Both older men; sent them upstairs.

One emphysema: Elderly man who left New York and thought he'd feel better here, but who finds himself choking on bad smog days. Gave him aminoph and O_2.

Three bronchial asthma cases: Two women, one boy. The women got aminophyllin from me. It still gives me enormous satisfaction to see them start to breathe easier soon as the stuff goes in the vein. Rog gave the boy adrenalin.

Two coronaries: Both older men, handled by Kurt and sent upstairs. Neither was in failure.

One woman who fell: She thought her ribs were fractured. They were neg.

One common cold.

One arm laceration: A long cut and a long tedious suture job.

Six hand lacerations (including fingers): Equally shared and sutured by the three of us.

One ring on index finger: Had to be sawed off by Rog, who is good with tools.

Two fish hooks in hands: I cut the hubs off and pushed them through. Very easy work in view of the anxiety it relieves. Kids are nearly always so terrified when they're hooked on something or something is hooked on them. I've seen more panic in fish hook cases than in real serious stuff.

One hematoma under index fingernail: Drilled by Kurt.

Three possible ankle fractures: X-rayed and strapped as sprained ankles by Kurt.

Six leg and foot lacerations: Four required sutures by Rog and me.

Two kids with rusty-nail foot-puncture wounds: Antitet by Logan.

One fourteen-year-old girl who thought her heart was going too slow: Pulse was 72.

One possible perforated duodenal ulcer: Definitely an acute belly. Guy seemed very sick, so upstairs stat!

One A.P.: A young woman with a hot belly like a rock, rebound, high white count, the works. Sent her upstairs.

One renal stone: Demerol by Logan as directed by me.

Two car accidents: Seven people brought in with contusions, ecchymoses, and a variety of general lawsuit-type complaints. A total of two real injuries, one requiring attending (fractured patella) and one requiring suturing of forehead. But I count this as seven because they all took much of our time and energy in examinations. I was also called upstairs to start an I.V., but I'll allow this one gratis. I visited Sailor and the carpenter, as did Kurt and Rog. This doesn't count.

So we had a total of eighty-four cases before I left. The nurses prepared them all, and together we did the work. Eighty-four is a pretty average day (there have been hundred-plus ones), and looking them all over I guess nothing very unusual happened. Just a hard-working, prosaic, predictable kind of a day. Sometime soon the shit will surely hit the fan. Am I getting so matter of fact? I don't think so. Looking for excitement? Could be!

I think the major anxiety comes from handling:

1. Kids, who, wrapped like mummies in blankets so that we can do the necessary, become hysterical and get to us.

2. Coronaries and C.V.A.s, because of the gravity of the things.

3. People in shock, because they can go down and out if they aren't treated stat.

The major time and hard work—it's real labor, and fatiguing as hell—is the suturing.

The major pains in the ass are writing up the charts and doing clinic work like physicals on people who ought to

be seeing private M.D.s or who ought to be coming around
to the clinic during regular hours. But of course many of
these people are sick, scared, and penniless. They have no
money for a private M.D. and are scared to wait for the
clinic to see them during regular hours. We ought to have
some kind of twenty-four-hour clinic for non-emergency
cases. This would take a lot of scut work off the E.R.

Just before I left, Morgan came in and told us that we
were wasting a lot of bandage. We now use elastic stuff
almost exclusively, and I suppose it is pretty expensive. I
have to admit that this is an area of great failing on my
part, and so I leave most dressings to Logan. Mine go out
looking pretty sloppy and bulky. I'm just not a good ban-
dager. Reminds me of my father back in the store. He'd
keep rewrapping a little finger cut until the guy walked
out looking as though he'd had major hand surgery. Is
that where I got a taste for all this—from my drugstore
beginnings? Maybe there *is* an early childhood reason for
everything!

Smithson has been hanging around here quite a bit lately
and I suddenly realized—I'm really slow in this department—that the crazy bastard is trying to make Logan.
He's going to get his ass shot off by John for sure. I have
a not-so-secret hope that Logan will really tell him off. But
she won't, because she goes about her business looking like
she doesn't know he's alive. How the hell does he go for
her? She's pretty, but like a piece of ice. I guess for these
kinds of guys it's the challenge—another notch. Is this
compensation for homosexual fear? Sounds too pat. Maybe

his screwing is like my eating, a response to fatigue and anxiety. I'm down to 253—got to keep trying!

Early this A.M. a twenty-seven-year-old woman was brought in off the coast highway with the worst lacerated face I've ever seen. She actually went through the windshield and was thrown out of the car onto the road. It's simply amazing that she wasn't killed and, as a matter of fact, aside from her face and multiple contusions she sustained no other major injuries. I consider the injury to her face major. It was more than lacerated—it was macerated, a terrible hodgepodge of deep lacerations, bruised burnt skin, fractured nose. Awful. Fortunately, she hadn't lost too much blood and she wasn't in shock. She kept asking to look at herself in a mirror, a request that of course we stalled off. We just held her face together with sterile wet pads and called Peter Davis, the attending plastic surgeon. When he looked at her he didn't seem particularly perturbed—it was almost as though he was examining her face for an elective nose job in his office. But he did examine every aspect of her injury and gave her as thorough a total physical exam as I've seen. After she went upstairs, he told us that she wouldn't look the same as before but that she'd come out just fine. Davis has a reputation for having done all kinds of facial reconstructions during the War, and I suppose these things are all relative. He reviewed her injuries with us and the amazing thing is that she was not terribly hurt, in either the irreparable sense or in terms of danger to her life. How she could get so badly mauled and not have any eye or serious head involvement—

let alone a facial bone, limb, or neck fracture—is pure miracle. One of the big pluses in her favor, Davis pointed out, was the fact that although she was badly bruised, lacerated and macerated, she had lost very little deep skin. He said that he didn't think any grafts would be necessary and told us that the age-old rule applies here as everywhere else in medicine: the less intervention the better.

Now, here is something I cannot see myself doing: plastic surgery! I don't know why, but it gets to me, I mean seeing and working on people without faces, etc. I remember this guy presented to us in med school, who had half a face missing as the result of a long-neglected basal cell epithelioma. This kind of thing gets to me. Is it anxiety related to loss of identity feelings? Here I am, going into psychiatry—the business of really tampering with people's identities on the deepest level—and I'm shook up about fooling with their physical-surface stuff. Anyway, when this woman next looks at herself, I hope she likes whom she sees! Maybe that's the answer to most things: if we like ourselves, perhaps surface phenomena then don't really count for all that much.

Today was the day for terrible things, though Davis didn't consider that woman's face terrible. We got the victims of a very bad two-car accident in Benedict Canyon. Everyone was dead except one little six-year-old girl. The driver of the other car—and this child's mother, father, older brother and sister—were all dead. The other guy mashed them coming from the other direction, and he reeked from booze. Aside from a small hematoma on her upper mid-forehead, the child had no injuries at all. She had apparently been sleeping throughout the whole thing and still had no idea what had happened. She seemed rather hazy to me, and I was afraid of concussion, but then we realized that she was just sleepy. The accident, as horrible as it was, had not fully awakened her. The police came with an aunt and uncle who signed against our advice and took her home. As a rule of thumb, we suggested she be observed upstairs for twenty-four hours, but they said they felt she needed them at home more. I can't blame them, and thank God they seemed like very nice people. I could tell they were having a hell of a time to keep from coming apart. The woman was the dead woman's sister, and every time she looked at the child she became racked with sobs and ran into a side room. When I looked at her and the child, I had to turn away, too. Even now I can't keep the tears from my eyes. The child asked for her mother several times, and we easily distracted her with candy. Even Logan was red-eyed and shaky. How terrible for that child—catastrophic. What can I say? Life is tenuous—of course it's tenuous. It's Goddamned ephemeral! But the great tragedy is the child's loss—the victims are the living people the dead leave behind. I suppose I identify with the child. The idea of the sudden loss of everyone I love, all in one shot, is too much for me to really conceptualize in my guts. Yet it could happen. Anything could happen—at any time! There's a lot of drunken driving here in southern California. This accounts for a large percentage of the worst accidents I've seen. The cops have come in to the E.R. and given balloon tests and the penalties are rough but it doesn't seem to stop anyone. I don't suppose punishment, or fear, stops any abnormal psychiatric process. Am I angry at this drunk driver who killed four innocent people and himself and left a little girl alone in the world? I'm not aware of it. I suppose it's hard to be pissed off at a dead man, and my feeling goes beyond rage. I guess I feel numbed, numbed and hurt and disgusted with the senselessness and the brutality of it all. The automobile is a great invention, but it will probably kill us all one day. I can see some exploratory archaeologists from another planet a half million years hence coming across stacks of rusted autos. They'll say, "This is the monstrous artifact that killed and supplanted the species called Homo sapiens." They won't know that we invented the monster ourselves. By the way, the smog was very bad today and even reached our neck of the woods. Morgan suggests that in part it's undoubtedly due to the traffic—automobiles again. Hang around here much longer and cars will be my greatest enemy.

Another kind of horror came in tonight—as a matter of fact there were several horrors, small but nevertheless lousy. One was quite literally lousy.

A man came in, dressed in rags, who looked like he was starving to death. He said there was nothing wrong with him except that he was hungry. This we all consider a real emergency! We loaded him up with sandwiches and stuff and got a huge food packet from the kitchen and gave it to him. Surprisingly, Logan never said boo—she actually cooperated. Another thing: she told Smithson off this A.M., really sharply—and threw him out of the joint! If I'm not careful, I might start liking her. Anyway, while this guy was eating (and I never saw such eating before—in this day and age, to see a man starving, whatever the reason!), we noticed him scratching. We looked him over with the eye magnifying glass. He was loaded with body lice—pediculosis. We got blue ointment from the pharmacy, told him how to use it, and sent him on his way with his food. Logan washed and disinfected everything he'd touched, might have touched and hadn't touched. We all took turns and ran off to take showers, but I still feel itchy as hell and haven't stopped scratching.

The night of horrors continued. A man came in who had been in a razor fight. We all took turns for about two hours suturing him up. He was lacerated in every conceivable place, including one long cut clean across his belly that fortunately never penetrated down beneath the abdominal fat layer. Well, we thought we were all through with him, and he got up from the treatment table—and there on the table was half a buttock. It must have been sliced through and his sweat made it stick to the table. Worst of all he started to bleed like a stuck pig. We used pads, Gelfoam—the works. There was nothing to suture, just one big ooze. We thought of sewing the half buttock back on and consulted Morgan, but he vetoed it. After quite some time we got it to stop bleeding by applying heavy pressure for about an hour. We had him sit on a heavy gauze pack that we improvised. We finally bandaged him up with Furacin and a load of packing and told him to report to the clinic in the A.M. We threw away the buttock, which (and I know this is coarse and disgusting) weighed about one and a half pounds. Here is a man who could literally have had his ass handed to him.

The last horror episode was a dart-in-eye case. The kid was about twenty years old and terrified of going blind. His fear was justified, and the reassurance I gave him stuck in my throat. He got in the way of a dart that penetrated his left eyeball. He pulled it out himself as soon as it happened and had no idea how far it penetrated. He was in deadly pain, so I gave him a quarter-grain of M.S., which relieved him considerably. I called Jack Stamm, our best eye attending and chief of the ophthalmology service and clinic. We were fortunate to get him at home, and he came right over. The globe was punctured, ruptured, and full of blood. The whole eyeball looked like a crenated erythrocyte. It was pushed in, as though the air had been let out. Stamm had us give him T.A.T. and penicillin, and then sent the kid upstairs. We called up to prepare the O.R. stat! He had Logan keep calling the kid's parents. He told us the eye was destroyed and that it ought to be enucleated immediately. He said that the great danger was that the other eye would turn sympathetic and that he would lose both.

I must say this is another thing I discovered I would not care to do: an eye enucleation. The whole concept of removing an eye bothers me. Yet I suppose I could do it, if the chips were down. God, the unnecessary messes people get themselves into. What's with us, anyway? Is this some kind of urge to self-destruction, Freud's death instinct? Hanging around here, it begins to seem possible. But it's too pessimistic—I refuse to believe it! I believe people are self-destructive, but I don't think self-destruction is instinctive. More likely it's due to immaturity, lousy judgment, carelessness, feeling omnipotent and mostly, probably, a result of self-hate (à la Karen Horney). I hope the kid's other eye is O.K.

Went up to see Sailor and Carpenter (as we now call Madden's compound-fracture guy). Sailor's legs are healing fine, and he's off antibiotics. Carpenter has a good deal of pain, an elevated temp, 102°, and obvious infection. But he expects to walk out of here. I hope he's not disappointed. Why the difference in healing between these two guys? Does being unconscious help healing? Nonsense! Older age and poor circulation don't help, but it's mostly that lousy soil—he's bound to be infected and an osteomyelitis with weird organisms can be one hell of a mess to clean up. Anyway, they did an open reduction and I understand Madden scraped the bones much more than usual. He's draining openly, and the smell of his room reminds me of when Sailor was still downstairs. Well, Sailor healed— maybe Carpenter will, too.

An attractive thirty-eight-year-old woman came in today with a "bad backache" and told us that she'd fallen and thought that maybe she cracked a few ribs. Kurt examined her thoroughly and found nothing wrong with her ribs but thought that she had considerable upper abdominal tenderness and much muscle-guarding. He had a hunch and got a flat plate (maybe he *did* work as a G.P. in Germany and was just very frightened when he first came here) of her abdomen. His hunch turned out right: Morgan read the plate and concurred with Kurt. They were fairly sure she had a ruptured spleen that was bleeding under the capsule and had not yet come apart. There was no time to lose, because once the capsule went the woman would die either of bleeding, peritonitis, or paralytic ileus—or all three. To say the least, time was of the essence, and yet we would have felt better about the diagnosis if we'd had a history more consistent with it. Morgan arranged for her to be a service case, had her sign the necessary forms, and had Logan call in the attending surgeon on call to assist him in the O.R. When we explained how serious the whole business really was, the patient finally capitulated.

We already had her typed and cross-matched and had whole blood going into her. I guess the sight of herself getting transfused brought the reality and seriousness of it smack home to her more than anything we said. She told us that her husband had had a few drinks—"he really didn't mean it"—pushed her to the floor, and kicked her in the belly. This is all Morgan needed. She had a splenectomy within the hour, and Morgan said that the capsule was on the verge of exploding just as they got the damn thing out. Writing this now seems terribly melodramatic, but the fact is that Kurt-the-former-Nazi's hunch saved this woman's life. Had we let her walk out, she would surely have died.

I must say, I've been feeling less tired since the Silent One arrived. He's a strange man; it's impossible to get him to say anything at all. But he's a good worker.

My weight is down to 241—only 41 pounds to go!

I think it was William Osler who said, "Please God, when I go don't take me through the kidney." I really don't know how painful death-dealing kidney disease is. I've had practically no experience with it. But I've seen a number of people with urinary retention and also several passing kidney stones. I saw one of the latter today. The textbook description is absolutely valid! I don't think I've ever seen people in so much pain as when passing a stone. This man today looked pale as a sheet and almost couldn't talk from the agony he felt. He managed to say that it was the "deepest" kind of pain he ever felt. He's already had an I.V.P. and is under the care of a urologist, so he knew that the diagnosis is renal colic. He says the stone was last visualized at the juncture of the ureter and the bladder. We gave him Demerol, and he sees his M.D. in the A.M.

I guess the whole pain-tolerance and sensitivity thing is a mystery. I've seen people walk in here in excruciating conditions in no great overt discomfort. Others with something relatively minor climb the walls. How much of it is a question of psychological approach to being sick, hurt, and in pain? I suppose fear and panic play a large role, though maybe hysteria is a good outlet and a relief. Those that grit their teeth certainly don't feel it any less. Maybe it's a question of inherited sensitivity, an inborn threshold to painful stimuli. More and more I think it has little or nothing to do with courage, manliness and all that cultural hokum. And more and more I have respect for people who yell out when they hurt. This seems appropriate and human. The gritting-teeth business seems like a phony John Wayne, pretentious affectation. If and when, I hope I have the guts to scream my head off.

Funny that I wrote of my feelings about pain yesterday. Today I found out what a Huk spear is. The Huks are apparently a tribe of fierce people who live in the Philippines and who harassed the other Filipino people before the War and the Japanese during the War. Well, one of their weapons is a spear, a real cute number. It consists of a bamboo shaft about four feet long attached to a two-foot iron bit that comes to a sharp point. This bit has four surfaces and is loaded with inch-long barbs that protrude from every millimeter of all its surfaces at a 45° angle in both

directions. There must be a hundred of these fish-hook type
protrusions on one spear:

This is a poor drawing because it shows only two surfaces
and there are four of them. How do I suddenly know all
this? A twelve-year-old boy walked in with one today. His
older brother brought it home from the Philippines at the
end of the War.

It was 4 P.M. and the E.R. was absolutely quiet. One of
those rare afternoon lulls; no customers. This medium-
sized, rather thin boy walked in alone, calm as you please
—supporting the bamboo shaft with his two hands, the
iron bit and all of its hooks stuck through his mouth and
coming out the other side of his neck. He was impaled on
this thing through the mouth above the tongue—with about
three inches of it protruding from his posterior neck. Mi-
raculously there was very little blood. He had somehow
missed the innumerable vital structures in the throat and
neck. He could have and should have at least nicked a
jugular, carotid, the spinal cord, and column (the thing
came out just left and lateral to the column). Christ, I remember the dissection of the neck back in Popoff's class in
Lausanne, and a mass of major nerves, glands, vessels—the
thyroid, parathyroids, etc., are located in this region. And
the thing is, this kid was in no distress at all—utterly calm
and cool. His brother came in a few minutes later, a guy
about twenty-five and he was absolutely frantic. We found
out that the kid lives two blocks from here and walked over

alone. With the help of the brother we pieced together what must have happened. The spear had been standing point up against the wall of a room the kid was playing in. He ran toward the wall, the floorboards were loose, the spear fell forward and he impaled himself through the mouth. Amazing how these freak things happen, and yet the more time I spend in the E.R. the less amazing or freakish anything seems.

We sat him on a chair, started a plasmoid I.V., gave him T.A.T., penicillin, and M.S. (though there was no evidence of shock—B.P. was normal—or pain). We held him still, though he made no move to move, and called Morgan. Interesting thing about this is that the boy, Allen, seemed bright, and his brother confirmed that he's a smart kid— yet he wasn't perturbed in the least. He was concerned and listened and obeyed what little we told him—not to move, etc.—but he evidenced no fear at all. Of course the M.S. helped, and made him sleepy at once. As soon as Morgan got down we sawed off the bamboo section, which immediately made the whole thing look less grotesque.

Of course it was obvious that this thing couldn't be snipped off like a fish hook and pushed through. He was hooked on Christ knows how many barbs going in both directions. Morgan and Logan arranged for films over in main X-ray and started to call up consultants—and I mean consultants. He must have arranged for an immediate meeting of ten different guys. Of course, my mind wandered to L.U.P., who also had every prof in the area in on her case. But this one was different. There was Madden, a neurosurgeon, a dental surgeon, a head and neck surgeon, Johnson, Aiken, and Peter Davis. I guess ten is an exaggeration —this makes seven. Later on Morgan said that he counted

sixteen barbs on the film and that they were practically
wrapped around nearly every vital structure in the neck.
He said they'd have to do extensive surgery to get the
thing out, involving dissection through the mouth as well
as from the outside through the lateral neck. Dr. Ralph
Watkins, a head and neck man from U.C.L.A., will operate. Davis, the plastic man, will first-assist. Morgan will
second-assist, and the others will be there on tap. Anyway,
they expect to do the job some time tonight. This is one I
have no desire to be in on. It is going to be long, arduous,
and very touchy. Oh shit! The real truth is I *can* see myself
there. I mean I just had a fantasy of doing this kind of
work, and I've got to cut it out. Is this more of the glory-
fantasy thing Horney writes about?

They operated late last night, and he's doing O.K. I went
in to see the kid, and of course he's all swathed in dressings so I couldn't see a thing. He's getting his nourishment
via Levine and I.V. tubes, but Morgan says this kind of
kid will probably be back to normal eating very quickly.
He said it was a superb neck anatomy lesson and beautiful
surgery. Watkins and Davis were brilliant. The thing took
six hours of meticulous and innovative work. They did
minimal damage. The kid is a perfectly healthy boy and
should heal well and quickly. He will probably be out of
here with drains out in no time at all. Davis says there
will be minimal scarring. There is concern about edema
around vital structures from the surgery, but they have
several drains in, have given him new enzymes that draw
off fluid, and it will be O.K. Morgan went on to describe

the whole procedure, but I got tied up with a suture job of my own and didn't hear it. What's the point, anyway? I'm just glad Allen will be O.K.

One of the specials on Sailor swore that he mumbled something today. We all ran up like lunatics, but there was no change at all. Reflexes, etc., are exactly as before. Did it really happen, or was it wishful thinking on her part? She must have been imagining.

Thank God (for a change) that there's such a thing as brilliant surgery, because there's some awful botchery around that passes for surgery. They called me up to the O.R. today (the residents on surg were sick) to assist a surgeon, so called. I subsequently found out he's known as Shaky Al. It was a cholecystectomy on a very fat woman. I guess I resent the whole thing because 1. I'm supposed to be on E.R. and I hate to go up and be a flunky in the O.R. for some guy who is lousy at his job; 2. I don't like to be part of a crummy enterprise even though I don't really have much choice; and 3. I'd just as well not stimulate in any way my interest in surgery because my psychiatric mind is made up! I suspect 3. carries the most weight.

This surgeon is called Shaky because he shakes! He's about fifty-five, sixty years old, and I suspect he has a mild Parkinson's. Regardless of diagnosis, he does have one hell of a tremor. Truth is he seemed to know his business quite thoroughly, but he had a hell of a time doing whatever it

was he had to do. There were several times during the procedure when he had me do things that definitely don't fall
into the province of an assistant. When I say he "had me
do," I mean just that: at various points he actually held my
hands and guided them through several manipulations. To
top it off, this woman had an empty sack of flesh that hung
forward and laterally from her abdomen. Obviously as
fat as she was she must have recently lost a hell of a lot of
weight. After the gall bladder was finally out he said he
had promised to get rid of this sack for her and proceeded
to amputate it. Well, the gall bladder had taken about three
hours, but the other Goddamned mess took another two
hours. Why? Because she bled like absolute crazy and went
into shock twice. We could have used a second assistant,
but there were only the two of us. Fortunately, the anesthe-
tist, a new guy whom I'd never seen before, was very good
and had plenty of blood going into her the whole time. I
don't know how the hell we did it, but when we finished
she looked pretty good—sans that big empty sack yet—a
reward, I suppose, for all the confidence she ever showed
in Shaky. Jesus, I just have to lose weight before I get so
old that my skin loses its elasticity! In any case, it's a Goddamned shame this s.o.b. is allowed in the O.R. I suppose
I'm being high-handed, but it's really pretty lousy, and I
state this here and now: I will not assist this guy again,
even if they throw me out! Let them just try. Frankly, I'm
still good and pissed off about the $1,000, but that's nei-
ther here nor there. Something else pisses me off. Madden
calls Morgan by his first name, Dave. He calls the rest of
us in the E.R. "Doctor"—just "Doctor." The son of a bitch
manages to say and use this so-called title with utmost
contempt. Even worse, it lumps us all into an amorphous

mass. I'll bet the s.o.b. doesn't even know our names. I've been here almost a year and this bastard still gives me this impersonal "Doctor" routine. I've hardly known Mank more than several weeks, and he calls me Ted. Maybe psychiatrists are generally more human and less full of shit. I hope so!

Speaking of pain again, a forty-two-year-old man came in tonight who is in deadly pain for which there is no surgical cure or sustained medical relief. His doctor called ahead and asked us to please tide him over with a stiff M.S. shot and a fistful of Demerol pills. He has multiple myeloma, and it's reached the stage where he has almost constant severe leg pain that gets much worse at night. When the man arrived we did as his doctor requested, immediately, but it wasn't only because the man was in severe pain or as a courtesy to his M.D. It was because we were in the presence of a devastating and hopelessly incurable malignant disease. This man was completely wasted: he had the look and smell of death, and it made us feel frightened, inadequate, and helpless. It brought the whole E.R. atmosphere, dynamism, and *raison d'être* down into the dirt. The bright, light warm place where we worked small but highly effective medical and surgical miracles momentarily become a morgue for the hopelessly living dead.

Much as we sympathized, we could hardly wait to relieve him and get him out, a feeling very much like the desire to get a foreign body out of a healthy eye. It was really amazing how Logan, Roger, and me practically met him at the door, did the necessary, and got him out before he could spoil our rosy picture of ourselves. I guess I feel badly, as if in a way we were contributing to the burial of a man who is still alive enough to experience severe pain:

we already saw him as dead! The truth is—I didn't realize
any of this until several minutes ago—we were terrified
of contamination! If I told the others they'd call it psychiatric crap. But it's true—we were scared—because no
amount of denial changes the fact that the hangman also
dies.

Speaking of hangmen dying, I got a letter today that
upset me a great deal. Norm Trachtenberg, whom I went
to school with, has multiple sclerosis. Twenty-seven years
old, and this. But why am I so hit by the news? True, I've
known him for years, and I'm truly sorry. But here again
is the shock that neither youth nor an M.D. degree sets people apart at all. The hangman indeed dies! There is no
protection, no insurance, no security—not much else than
this very moment. This whole life thing is just too Goddamned tenuous, and being a doctor and being in the middle of the fire gives momentary illusions of cool, safe places.
But Norm, among others, proves that training and degrees
don't change people's vulnerability one iota. I say this in
part because more and more I notice in our conversations
and in those of older M.D.s around me this referral to
"they" and "them" and "we" and "us" as though real
differences exist. Well, all this is I suspect some magical
attempt to believe that auto accidents, myeloma, M.S., coronaries, etc., can't really get to the super people who treat
them all. Maybe this kind of feeling is necessary in order
to go on being effective while constantly working with
grim pathology. But it is, of course, pure hokum. There
ain't no *we* and *them,* only *us* and some of-us foolishly
making like there's *them.*

Everybody is sick with this virus thing that's going around except Logan, Mary, Morgan, and myself. Wonder how we are going to manage, and I hope to hell I don't come down with it.

As a result of this I worked my ass off today. Morgan pitched in as much as he could, but mostly he was needed upstairs. I had no chance at all to visit Carpenter or Sailor, but Morgan says nothing has changed with them. Fortunately, it's been relatively quiet—mostly routine stuff.

Everybody is still sick and Madden, still with the "Doctor" crap, asked me to take over. "Take over," I came to find out, means to be on duty—all the time, with intermittent cat naps—until the others can come back. I understand this virus thing makes for some pretty high temps and is running every G.P.'s ass off throughout the state. Madden said that he personally promises me recompense —and I here quote: "You will be amply rewarded." Now, just what does that mean? I still have the $1,000 in mind, but I'm sure he doesn't, and I don't have the guts to ask him. Well, I can't very well say no. So I say yes, and he pats me on the back and says people from the floors will help from time to time. All this time he calls me "Doctor"— God forbid such familiarity as my actual name.

I need to eat; instead I sleep. That's not what I mean. I mean just the reverse—that's how tired I am. I guess this too is a Freudian slip—maybe I do prefer eating to sleeping. It hasn't even been so busy. I think just the knowledge that I can't sleep makes me feel tired, deprived, self-sacrificing, and hungry.

I managed to sleep in the side room for about two hours in the last twenty-four. We got busy as hell and a couple of girls from upstairs came down to help. Morgan must have been down here for ten hours, and the two of us had a hell of a time handling it all. Betty Smith and these gals from upstairs can't hold a candle to Logan. There's something for you: nurses work eight hours—they're considered human; we work *all* hours—no wonder we get to feel we are a species apart.

If not for Morgan I'd drop dead. We both look ready for the undertaker. I've never been so tired in my life. Screw it, I just can't write another word—even though we had a few interesting things happen today.

Morgan hasn't been down here in twenty hours; he's been stuck upstairs. I'm going to drop dead for sure. When I try to sleep I hallucinate ambulance sirens and jump up with a start—battle fatigue? One gratification: I've been eating like crazy and surprised as hell to find I'm at 248. It must be the lack of sleep keeping it down, the many extra hours of full metabolism.

Smithson got over the virus—he must have caught it early, and he's been down here a good deal. He's quite capable. I was able to sleep about four hours in the last twenty-four. This sleep thing: too bad we need it at all or at least we should be able to push a button and fall asleep instantly. I've got a long list of complaints about the so-called human condition.

A woman came in today with a windshield wound of the axilla. Her entire left armpit was laid open, beautifully incised so that we could see the contents hanging there as though they were on exhibit. Nerves, vessels, fat tissue, lymphatics, were all exposed and fortunately none of them seemed damaged. Neither Smithson nor I wanted to take the responsibility for closing this one, and we couldn't get Morgan, so we finally got Madden. He went over the area completely, using a magnifying glass looking for glass particles, and carefully tested her arm and finger function. (Frankly, I was just too tired to think of this.) He finally closed her up and really did an A-1 job. I'd never really seen him do very much before. He said we did right to call him because this kind of closure is tricky even without underlying structure involvement. In an axillary laceration as deep and extensive as this (arm to chest), anything but perfect closure could impair movement later on and produce pain for a lifetime. I think he said something about "neuromas." Insane thing is, this woman swears she was trying to park and, going only about five miles an hour, somehow managed to go into a concrete post. Fortunately, her neck and head were O.K., no whiplash. Madden praised us for getting films on her neck and gave us a small sermon on lawsuits, which we had heard before, and which was all I needed to put me right back into my exhaustion haze. I have to admit that these kinds of crazy "live dissections" still get to me. Truth is, I hate to look at them. Maybe I've got some kind of emotional need to keep things on the surface, to leave deeper stuff alone. Anyway, I'm too tired to give a damn.

Thank God the Silent One and Logan are back, because I've been going around in a stupor. I'm just not good at turning on fifteen-minute sleep intervals on command. Throughout some of this I notice there are times when my mind is blank. Other times it races ahead with all kinds of disconnected thoughts, words, memories, and fantasies. Maybe this is a special craziness associated with fatigue. What if that's what sleep is all about? Perhaps we do it because we have some kind of inborn neurological need to dream, and go on and dream anyway when we can't and don't sleep. Maybe this is what craziness is—awake dreaming.

Last night in the middle of my "awake-dreaming craziness," (that's another thing about sleeplessness—it gets harder to tell what really happened and what was really a dream) a woman came in to buy a penicillin shot. All I remember is that I started out calmly explaining why we don't sell shots, but that I could examine and treat her. We got into a hell of a screaming thing, and I threw her out. Seems she was yelling something about suing us. Well, let her—screw her! Screw Madden! Screw Quistle! Fuck them all!

We're back to full staff—thank God again—and I'm still alive and still 247 pounds for all my ordeal. Madden called up and told me to take two full days off starting tonight. Maybe this is the "reward." Anyway, I'm taking three big shots of Scotch here and now and sacking out stat!

I slept eighteen hours, for the first time in my life. Still feel groggy but O.K.

Today I got my "reward." Madden thanked me, still using the "Doctor" shit, slipped me a check as if he was doing something illegal, and whispered that this came out of his own pocket. When he left and I looked (too self-effacing and too proud to look when he gave it to me), I saw the big news. Sixty and 00/100 dollars—that's it! Screw 'em all!

Being on twenty-hour hours a day for nearly a week, practically alone, has left me no thinner than before. I'm back to 250 again. But it has given me a certain confidence —confidence and $60. I'm pretty good at this E.R. thing. I really believe I actually did much of it sleepwalking. Anyway, it gives me a sense of accomplishment that feels very good. I've got more stamina than I thought. I know it's pretty silly and childish, but it does make me feel a little heroic. I suppose it sort of fits in with the kid fantasies I used to have of being the self-sacrificing doctor and all that.

Horney's neurotic glory? Maybe, but also a feeling of what I suspect is genuine self-satisfaction, that I hope I can go on owning in the future. Maybe this is pretty damn arrogant on my part, but I'm really beginning to think that I've discovered my second big talent. The first, which I discovered in medical school, was a genius for gin rummy —which is boring and useless. This, the second, may be E.R. work—which I suppose will be useless also. I just hope the third turns out to be psychiatry.

Allen, the boy of Huk-spear fame, went home today. I saw him just as he was leaving. They had him in a wheel-chair going out to the curb, which is strictly routine; he seemed fine. His face is still completely swathed, but Morgan says he's in amazingly good condition. There will be very little scarring and no loss of any function at all. Human beings have amazing healing power—the ability of protoplasm to bounce back! It's certainly true of Sailor, whose legs are in great shape. But Carpenter is in trouble. He has a bad osteo and doesn't seem to be healing at all. There's some talk about sending him home anyway. I guess there's no point in keeping him here. He can be treated on an out-patient basis. Even with hospitalization insurance this place gets pretty expensive, I suppose.

Speaking of legs, today Johnson called us up to see a Poor's machine in action. I never heard of the damned thing till today. Apparently nobody but Johnson had either. He had this thing shipped in from San Francisco and he says it may be the only one in the state. I guess a Dr. Poor invented the thing. It consists of a series of hollow tubes that wrap around the legs and are hooked to a specially designed air machine. This machine inflates and deflates the tubes rhythmically and sequentially, producing strong pressure waves like continuous massages down both legs. The purpose is to supplement circulation of the lower limbs from the outside in order to compensate for impaired natural circulation. Johnson's patient is a forty-year-old woman with very severe impairment. She was unconscious, comatose, had obviously sustained a severe C.V.A. Johnson told us that his patient has a long history of severe rheumatic heart disease, had blown a C.V.A. four days earlier and developed cold legs two days later. He says that his opinion is that she is showering emboli (from an old endocarditis), which accounts for her C.V.A. and her legs. He feels certain that she had an embolus, now turned thrombus, lodged in the bifurcation of the common iliacs. He hopes that the Poor machine can help save her legs until she is in some kind of shape to withstand surgery.

Poor's machine couldn't do it. Rather than risk amputation, they operated, and actually managed to ream through a massive thrombus. Circulation in her lower legs is now O.K. and is getting continuous help from the Poor gadget —this a job for which it is adequate.

I think I'm over my big exhaustion; I'm now back to my "regular" fatigue. Some day in the future I'm actually going to feel really fresh—no fatigue. Weight, 248 pounds. The hell with it!

Sailor is O.K., but his mother and father were there today and they both suddenly look like very sad old people. I didn't know until today that Sailor is their only child.

The Poor machine woman died. The C.V.A. did its dirty work. Interesting gadget, the Poor machine.

Carpenter went home today. He will see Madden outside. His leg is in pretty bad shape—there's no evidence of the infection clearing up. You just don't stick bones in the ground.

This P.M. we had a woman in badly mauled by her own dog. She looked pretty awful. She had multiple contusions, lacerations, and half an ear nearly bitten off. This dog, a chow that she'd had for four years, was sitting on her lap, nice and playful. He suddenly got his toenail caught in her sweater and couldn't extricate himself. They both went into a panic and he bit hell out of her. She says the more entangled he got the more he attacked her, apparently having completely forgotten who she was. By some miracle he finally sprang loose. She's really lucky to be alive. She had several dog bites on her neck, but he missed the jugular. She's sure the dog is not vicious, that it was purely a case of panic, but she's going to have him destroyed anyway. He's had rabies shots, so Morgan didn't feel that she needed inoculation, which is a mess in itself and can be dangerous as well. The first day I worked the E.R. full time, a young woman came in bitten by a stray dog who seemed frothy and strange and couldn't be found. At the request of her doctor we started her on the first of a series of fifteen shots that she would have to get intracutaneously. It's the first and only time I've given a shot into the skin of the abdomen. I've been told that rabies vaccine can cause encephalitis, so the decision regarding shots is not easy. Just before she left, the chow woman (how fast people become descriptive titles around here!) told us that as soon as the dog got off her sweater he recognized her again and wagged his tail as though nothing had ever happened. I have no doubt that panic can create temporary amnesia in animals as well as people.

Dreamed of Johnson's Poor machine woman last night and cried in my sleep. Why? I hardly knew her. This is one whom I'm sure I felt and feel relatively detached from. Maybe she reminded me of Mrs. James. Jesus—psychiatry should be a welcome haven from all this lousy maiming and dying!

A woman came in today who was sure she was dying but wasn't. Funny, because at one and the same time she told us that she has a long history of being a hypochon-driac and, more specifically, a cardiac phobic, and she is terrified that she is now having a "real heart attack." I say funny because self-knowledge as concerns her neurosis doesn't seem to help her in the least. She was hyperventilating like crazy and this, nearly making her pass out, had her convinced that the time had finally come, that her worst fears had been confirmed, that this indeed was a heart attack. I checked her over carefully. It's possible to be a cardiac phobic and still have a heart attack—I haven't forgotten Mrs. James. But this woman had nothing physically wrong with her whatsoever, except dizziness and a slightly rapid pulse from panic and hyperventilating. I tried talking to her and reassuring her, etc., but to no avail. I don't think she heard a word. Then I recalled Kurt's sterile-water placebo treatment, and I told her that I was going to give her a shot that would sedate and calm her so that she would feel much better and would realize that nothing was wrong except for nervous breathing. I gave her a shot and it worked like a charm. Nothing like piercing the skin and strong suggestion, because it worked as well as Luminal. Ten minutes later she listened and accepted the results of my examination and went home, saying (I quote): "Hope that the shot doesn't make me too sleepy to see Sid Caesar tonight!"

I did another and slightly deeper bit of psychotherapy tonight with a panicky fourteen-year-old boy who was sure he had a galloping case of V.D. We went into a side room where he showed me a slightly irritated penis. We sat and talked for half an hour. The irritation was obviously due to masturbation, and the fear of V.D. was due to guilt. This was a very bright and very ignorant kid as regards both masturbation and V.D. I elucidated both in detail and his change in mood was fantastic. His face really lit up when I said that everyone but everyone did it who was not having regular sex and even those who were did it sometimes too, and that it was not only harmless but even natural and good. We established rapport so well that he also confided in me that he was worried about the size of his penis. I assured him that his penis was absolutely normal in size and all other respects, and that size played a very small role in a happy sex life. I told him two stories: 1. How Popoff, my anatomy professor, introduced his lecture on the penis: "The average size of the erect penis is about six inches—Mrs. Popoff has had to be satisfied with four inches"; 2. A story I heard from a guy on internal medicine. His professor of GYN spoke about masturbation. One student came up after class and told the prof he had never masturbated. The prof said that he was sorry he had missed all that fun. Anyway, all this worked and the kid went out feeling fine. I suppose this is a form of psychotherapy, even if it doesn't have much depth or basis in psychoanalysis. It made me feel pleased with myself and good about psychiatry.

What is the hypochrondriac thing about anyway? Does it fill some kind of emptiness? Is it a form of denial? Is it a way of obfuscating whatever the real issue is, a way of avoiding or escaping the real problem? I'll have to wait for these answers, and God knows whether anyone knows. I wonder what percentage of regular medical practices is made up of hypochondriacs, and to what extent general practitioners and internists function as amateur psychiatrists? Maybe this is what makes them so hostile and estranged from professional psychiatrists—the inner knowledge that they are functioning in an area where they can only be second best.

I removed a corneal metal implant today. My ophthalmology prof was right—the cornea is really a tough piece of tissue. I had a hell of a time spudding this one out, but it finally came out O.K. There's really been a drop in industrial eye stuff lately. I guess the guys are finally wearing their goggles.

Madden came down high as a kite. The nurse had been right. He saw Sailor mumble. Nothing intelligible came out, but he moved his lips and definitely made some sounds. We're all excited as hell, and we broke a bottle out of somewhere and had a drink. Madden says he also moved his lips ever so slightly in response to pain (pinprick). We all ran up. He looks the same as before—no sound, nothing—but something is beginning to move in that head of his. Madden cautioned us to say nothing to his parents. Disappointment of this kind can be catastrophic!

We're still waiting, patiently, but Sailor's the same as before. He's just going to keep us waiting, I guess. Madden
says these cases are very erratic and strange, and he feels
that no intervention at all is what's indicated. At Madden's
request the navy sent over a neurologist for a consultation.
Madden says he thinks there are some neuro changes, but
he wouldn't swear to it. They don't want to do a spinal
tap or anything else. So things go on strictly status quo.

We made a brilliant diagnosis tonight, Rog and me. A
woman brought in a little three-year-old girl with a fecal
impaction who was obviously having a great deal of discomfort. This is the history we got: this child for the last
two months has been terrified of moving her bowels. She
walks about with her legs together, crying and in obvious
agony. When she finally moves her bowels, because there's
no longer any choice (about every five days) the accumula-
tion makes for a huge stool. Her pediatrician has had her
X-rayed and for a while thought she might have a borderline mega-colon (Hirschprung's disease), but this was ruled
out. The pediatrician now wants the child to have a
psychiatric consultation, which has not yet been done. Up
to today, the child has in each instance finally moved her
bowels, with the aid of mineral oil and rectal diathane
ointment. Today, though, was especially bad. The child
hadn't moved her bowels in six days and went about in
agony all day. Her mother couldn't contact the pediatrician
tonight and so she came here. We sedated the child with
a tiny dose of Luminal and then gave her a small ear-
syringe enema of warm oil and gradually worked this
hellish huge thing out. I thought we'd have to call a proc-
tologist, but it worked out O.K. The lesson I learned with
the sedated urinary-stone man came in very handy here. A

little sedation goes a long way, a lot further than restraints.
I can't stand the business of the wrap-around blanket
straightjacket we put on kids when we suture them, but
most of the time we just have no time to wait for sedation.
Anyway, this screaming girl immediately changed into a
beautiful, laughing, loving baby. Then it hit us, Rog and
me both at the same time. Is this mental telepathy or
common backgrounds for the moment on the same ex-
perimental wavelength? We asked the mother if the child
had had a stool analysis for parasites. She said there had
been some kind of analysis, but she didn't think anyone
ever mentioned a parasite analysis. We immediately sent
some of the stool upstairs to the lab and Rog put a piece of
Scotch tape across the child's anus and had the mother and
child wait in the waiting room. After a few hours we took
off the tape and examined it under the blood-lab micro-
scope. It was loaded with pinworms. We told the woman,
and told her to tell the kid's doctor and to get him to put
her on antiworm therapy and to call us in several days to let
us know how things were. We are sure we hit it and that
she will be O.K. A thing like this really makes it all seem
worthwhile. How come we made the diagnosis when more
experienced men failed? I think it's because we are less
than a year out of med school and still close to basics.
Without being arrogant, I hope, I think the thing to remember is to cover the simplest ground before going on to
more exotic and esoteric territory.

I had a dream in which I punched Sailor in the mouth. I
actually feel angry at him. I've been up there a dozen
times in the last few days—we wait and wait and *no*

dice! I guess I'm making a neurotic claim (Horney) that he owes me a response. It would be nice, though, if he spoke up. But there he lies, a silent organic factory again.

Today I learned about the relative value of "things." A woman came in with her hand and fingers caught in an elaborate kitchen appliance of some kind. Two fingers were cut deep, and she was bleeding badly. Well, I got out the hacksaw to get this thing off. Until that point she'd been utterly calm, but when she saw the hacksaw she got absolutely frantic. She pleaded with me to please get her out of this thing without cutting the appliance. I told her that it would be much more painful that way, but she went on and on to tell me that she didn't mind pain and to please save this lousy piece of metal. During all this we were wasting time and she kept bleeding. I finally told her there was no other way and I went ahead with the saw. When I finally got her out of it and was suturing her hand, she kept whimpering about the lousy appliance.

Today we had a very prissy single twenty-five-year-old girl in from an automobile accident. I mean Prissy with a capital P. She made a hell of a fuss about putting on an examining gown—our touching her, etc. She complained of pain on pressure over her pelvic girdle and we wanted to check her out on a possible cracked pelvis. Her films came back negative, but there smack in the middle of it all was a contraceptive diaphragm. The metal ring shows up perfectly on film. Of course we said nothing.

We had a moderate-sized earthquake last night. No one got hurt, but it was really scary. It makes for a very intense and acute attack of helplessness. When this building swayed up and back, all the medical expertise in the world seemed a bit unimportant.

We've had little tremors on and off for the last twenty-four hours. Several people came in afraid of heart attacks who were perfectly O.K.—physically, that is. Morgan says this is fairly typical "earthquake fever"—in short, anxiety attacks brought on by a sense of helplessness and sudden consciousness of mortality. He says that doctors get particularly busy following natural catastrophes of any kind. Aside from the town of Tahatchope, southern California is fortunately virtually untouched. They did find a crack running the whole height of the posterior wing of the building. Fortunately, this affected no one and can be repaired.

Madden came by and told us that Carpenter's leg looks like hell. The Huk kid is doing great. The drains were all removed.

The police brought two guys in tonight who had been in an "altercation." They had beat the hell out of each other. I always thought that the movie version of a fight was pure hokum—it seemed to me that a fist in the face must be enormously destructive. These two guys proved me right. Their faces were really mashed up—split lips, fractured noses, teeth out, and one guy has a severely fractured jaw. He's going to have a hell of a time eating or talking for a long while to come.

Sailor still insists on the deep freeze!

The pinworm child's mother called. She's absolutely fine! She's moving her bowels daily and even twice daily, and her movements are normal-sized. She thanked us profusely, and it was kind of embarrassing. She said that we restored her household and family to normalcy. Later on a kid delivered a big box of cookies from her with a warm wonderful note. Of course I've eaten at least a pound of them. Fattening but very good. What's a mere 255 pounds for a guy with a frame as big as mine? *Rien du tous!*

I like to think that our E.R. is the best equipped and best staffed in the country. Actually, I suspect that it does compare very favorably to most others. I've seen four others so far, two huge city hospital E.R.s and two in hospitals this size in New York. Ours is vastly superior in every way. I saw people waiting in the halls in the others for hours before anyone got around to them. But there's no point in criticizing them here. This is, after all, only a description or record diary of what goes on here, with me. Anyway, I suppose we could use a considerably larger place and at least three more doctors. We ought to be working fewer hours so that we'd be more awake and more efficient. Of course, there are rare and short periods of time when the place is empty and seems overequipped and overstaffed. I can recall at least ten different occasions when three or even four of us have worked on the same patient. I must also say that this was good for the patient. There's nothing wrong with a severely injured man getting blood pumped in by one guy, being sutured by two other guys, while one man attends to all of his vital signs, medication, and immediate management. But this is extremely rare, and the reverse situation is true only too often.

For example, tonight we got a five-car pile-up off the

coast highway, which has been more foggy than usual for this part of the state. There were sixteen patients in here from the pile-up at the same time, and Morgan, the Silent One, Rog and me and Kurt, plus four nurses from upstairs that I never saw before. We had every conceivable injury and two D.O.A.s. Four of them were in shock, half a dozen were badly cut up, and one man's nose was completely smashed. One's ribs were mashed in and we think she punctured her right lung (no breath sounds over right chest). There was a fractured humerus and a smashed patella and a crushed foot. One girl had a factured jaw. There was a possible fractured neck. One guy was gushing big bloody clots from his mouth and had that gray moribund look. The place seemed very chaotic, but at the same time it was not really too badly organized. Of course, a few people were quite hysterical, concerned only about other people they were with. We didn't care who came from which car, but they did. There were police all over the place. Like right out of a grade-B melodrama, we tried as usual to treat people with a sensible kind of priority. Of course, we treated anyone in shock first and got to the fractures and "smaller" stuff like lacerations later. In the middle of it we also got an overdose, a woman who was beat up and looked bad, and an old man who was cyanotic as hell and obviously having a coronary. I got busy with the guy, who was streaming blood clots out of his mouth. His blood pressure was down to almost nothing and he looked gray as death. More than that, he seemed to be choking on his own blood. Like out of that B movie, Morgan quickly looked him over (the man was fifty-five) and decided that he was moribund, probably a ruptured liver or some other irreversible damage to a vital organ. He didn't tell me to go on to someone else, but that was the implication. These are the tricky times, because everyone else was tied up and we were waiting for Madden and also Tracy, the chest surgeon, to arrive. It's this kind of thing that convinces me that we need a bigger place and staff. I guess enough is never enough. Anyway, without trying to give myself any heroic shit—not too much, anyway—this guy became a challenge of sorts. I must say my immediate clinical know-how was not one iota better than Morgan's. I too thought the guy had massive internal injuries and like the D.O.A.s that just came in he too would soon be dead. But I was hooked on him and just couldn't let go. At the same time I did feel a sense of guilt for not running over to someone else who obviously looked in much better shape and had a better chance of making it, even the overdose or coronary. I never worked my 250 pounds around so fast in my life. I was hollering orders to Liz on the coronary (O_2 and M.S.) and at the same time got Mary to bring over a suction machine and to keep sucking my hemorrhaging guy's pharynx out so that he didn't choke. Meanwhile I started plasmoid on both arms and pumped one furiously. Luckily Tracy came in then, and somehow he was caught by my patient, too, instead of the punctured lung he was called for. By this time I think I was getting more blood into him than Mary was getting out of him, because his color was improving radically. Tracy gave him a fast work-over and got a tracheotomy set and quickly trached him. His breathing improved 200 percent stat and his color turned quite normal. In no time he became conscious and seemed O.K. He was back from the dead. All this took about ten to fifteen minutes. Since he was breathing through his trache so beautifully now, we knew that the blood was coming from above and there was a good chance that his coma was due only to shock from blood loss. Tracy calmly looked down his throat, using the powerful lamp we use on eyes. He had his head almost down his throat, and bang! Just like that he snaps a hemostat on a big pharyngeal gusher. He tied it off and told me the guy was probably cured. He was! Trauma somehow caused this arterial hemorrhage, but he didn't even have an injury to any of his neck bones. The guy might have died from loss of blood and asphyxiation. Instead he was one of three people of that group who went home the same night they came in.

It was fairly quiet today, so I spent some time wandering around upstairs. I stopped in Sailor's room and he looked exactly the same.

Two cases up there got to me.

One is a case of trigeminal neuralgia. I can't remember if this is the same as tic douloureux. I'm just too tired and lazy to look it up now. Now I remember—of course it's tic douloureux! Anyway, this woman, sixty years old, has severe unrelenting pain all along the course of her left facial nerve. They've tried absolutely everything, all to no avail. They even tried alcohol injections, trying to destroy the nerve or ganglion, but no dice. Now they're talking of doing a prefrontal lobotomy, which may do it but which is radical as hell. It's liable to leave her rather vegetable-like. I spoke to her, and she seemed quite nice. She told me she's had the pain for years and just couldn't go on with it any longer. This kind of chronic thing must really wear people down. I wonder if psychotherapy of any kind can be helpful.

The other case was a forty-one-year-old woman with a melanoma in her iris. That is, she *had* a melanoma in her iris. They've already enucleated her eye. This was the first time I've heard of a melanoma in the eye—it can be anywhere on the skin, that I know, but I never heard of it in the iris. Of course, she won't make it. Jagger (my derm prof) called it the second most malignant tumor known to man. The first he said is known to women only: arrhenoblastoma. I still remember the young girl he presented to us, beautiful and healthy looking except for the pinhead lesion he removed from her thigh. Her groin was already infiltrated with metastases and six weeks later she was dead and full of lung melanoma. He called it the "great colonizer." Amazing how a little nothing nevus can turn bad and become a killer, sending colonies of itself all over the body. Jagger showed us lung slides full of nevus-like skin tissue from a primary lesion the size of two pinheads located on the heel. But the iris—that's a particularly sneaky place to hide. This woman seemed very bright. She knew that she had a nevus kind of cancer in the eye, but she thought she was absolutely cured and was "so, so grateful." I guess denial can keep you from greater craziness and even suicide.

I also heard parts of two lectures while I was up there. One was on esophageal C.A. The other was on general practice. In essence, the first amounted to the fact that esophageal C.A. is absolutely hopeless and produces a horrible death. Christ—the evils that can befall us are just too much. The essence of the second: get a patient and get her to like you and you will get her whole family as patients, especially if she's a loudmouth. This lecture should have been entitled "Medical Business," because that's what it was. But what am I feeling so high-handed about? Since I never have enough money, more and more I'm beginning to feel that doctors are entitled to a damn good living to compensate for earlier servitude.

Tonight, about seven, I saw the most severe case of anaphylaxis ever. This chef came in from one of the local swank country clubs. He was blown up, enormously red and balloon-like, itching furiously with huge red urticarial welts all over his body. Most important, he was drowning in his own fluid. His lungs were completely full. Fortunately, he was our only patient, so three of us worked on him at the same time. This kind of anaphylaxis can produce death in a matter of minutes, and on the other hand it is a completely reversible process—also in very short order. Fortunately, the one thing he didn't have was laryngeal edema. Well, we put tourniquets around his legs and arms and tilted his head down so that bleeding into peripheral tissues would not deplete his brain of fluid and cause further shock. We gave him a load of adrenalin to close his capillary beds and shot him full of I.V. and I.M. Benadryl and mercural hydrin (to help pee out the fluid). We then slowly gave him a dose and a half of I.V. aminophyllin plus O_2 by nasal catheter. In minutes his color got better and his breath sounds turned from gurgling water to air. By the time his private doctor arrived, he was out of the woods—still plenty swollen, but O.K. in the chest. His doc decided to keep him upstairs overnight. It will probably take a few days for all the tissue swelling to go down. Now hear this: this was an allergic response to crab meat. The chef knows that he's allergic to it. But he didn't eat it this time around—he knows better. This kind of histamine anaphylaxis has happened to him before and of course terrified him. All he did this time was touch the stuff—he was making crab salad—and apparently this was enough. That's what I call sensitivity! Later on Morgan told us that crab has a particularly high protein concentration—as does horse serum, I guess. I now see why we always skin-test with T.A.T. or other animal serum preparations. Morgan says there've been a number of deaths reported on allergy penicillin responses. We always ask if a patient is allergic to penicillin. Of course, it's not the first shot that does it; that only sets up the antibodies that go into active destruction in response to the second shot, even years later. I have a newfound respect for allergy. From now on any antibiotics I take have to be by mouth.

The chef came by this A.M. to thank us and invite us all to dinner at the club any time we care to drop by. We couldn't believe it was the same guy. His face is actually thin. I thought he had fat blubbery lips, but now I see they were full of fluid. He still itches a bit and is continuing on oral antihistamines, and I guess his skin swelling will go down still further. Country club dinners are all I need—I'm up to 253 again, and that's not allergic fluid of any kind. I'm allergic to food and my response is weight—fat weight!

There's a Dr. Robert Richardson who can drop dead stat! This morning, 3 A.M., I get called to see this son of a bitch's private patient. She had a breast cyst removed three weeks ago that's been infected and running pus ever since. Tonight she had a lot of pain, took the dressing off herself, looked at it for the first time, got terrified, called him. And this bastard sends her here, where I get woke up.

This son of a bitch, whom I never heard of, takes this woman's money and uses us as his auxiliary assistants free of charge because he wants to sleep. All of which she's not responsible for. I cleaned her up best I could and redressed the thing. We gave her some Luminal to calm her down and sent her home. The thing really looked awful! I wonder if it will ever heal. Reminded me of Carpenter. Hope he doesn't lose the leg.

We got a four-year-old kid with a head injury today. Cut-the-Cord Hauser, as he is now known, came in to examine her. She had bleeding out of her left ear and the films clearly demonstrated a skull fracture. The point I want to make here is that while this bastard is a pompous ass, the exam he gave her and the lecture he gave us as he examined her were nothing short of brilliant. I still hate this kind of inconsistency and still hate Hauser too, but I have to admit he seemed to know his stuff. Maybe he had a bad day the time Morgan thought he cut that cord, or maybe he's a crack neurologist, diagnostician, and teacher, but a lousy surgeon.

We also had a tough guy come in with a fish hook in his hand. He was huge, thirty-four years old, not drunk but with a definite boozy smell. He told us to be damned careful or he'd break up the place. Imagine the kind of s.o.b. who comes for help, then threatens the people who are trying to help him. Well, Logan made a phone call and next thing her boyfriend, John the cop, walks in, just as we got the hook out. He pulls this guy up by the arm and slaps him hard with his open palm across the face so the guy has a one-sided blush, and tells him to beat it fast before he locks him up. The guy just crumbled apologetically and practically crawled out. I hate to see anybody get hit, but

I must say this felt good. I suppose bullies are very frightened and fragile people underneath, but I still don't like them. We all went over and congratulated Logan and John.

Today we got a suicide (D.O.A.) by hanging. The guy looked terrible. What a cruel thing to do to oneself. The worst part—and this still gets to me and to all of us and always will, I guess—the guy was a doctor.

Morgan told us that the D.O.A. doctor yesterday came to California a few weeks ago from Detroit. He had a C.A. of the colon and recently had a colostomy, but apparently knew there were already some metastases elsewhere. So many people seem to come here to solve their problems and most problems just don't solve by changes in geography, let alone ones like this poor guy had. Would I want to die in this kind of circumstance? No! I'd want to live till the last second. But that's easy for me to say, not being in that kind of circumstance. But hanging—an overdose of M.S. is so much gentler. Maybe this was a way of expressing his rage—at the world, the human condition, and at himself for getting sick. Maybe doctors have a special pride (Horney) in not getting sick and magnified self-hate if they do get sick.

Today we saw a man who took his entire house apart—I mean wrecked it almost completely: broke up furniture, windows, everything. His wife told us that he is epileptic and this is the third time in two years this has happened. He went into a blind rage, seemingly precipitated by nothing at all, wrecked the place, and then passed out. Her doctor, an internist I don't know, told her to bring him here when he regained consciousness. I guess he thought he might need some help and was afraid to have him come to his office. Better to break up the E.R. than his joint, I suppose. The patient seemed kind of hazy, a little out of it, and said that he felt very weak and tired. He had no memory of being violent. The doctor came in and told us that the patient has a long history of epilepsy (since age fourteen—he's now fifty-four) and until recently has been well controlled on Dilantin and phenobarb. He said that they would try stronger stuff, but that if it didn't work they would have to hospitalize him. These psychomotor equivalents can be very dangerous. They then went home sans benefit of treatment by us. I remember reading a psychiatric case history of a man with psychomotor epilepsy who woke up, stabbed all the members of his family to death, and went back to sleep. Of course, 99 percent of epileptics fortunately have no such manifestations yet for many years were victims of prejudice and indiscriminately hospitalized along with psychotic patients for no rational reason at all. As a matter of fact, it's not so long ago that schizophrenia, general paresis, and epilepsy were all considered and handled as one illness. No one dreamed that G.P. was caused by *Treponema pallidum.* Someday we will find out that schizophrenia and psychosis are really fifty different diseases too. Also, not so long ago the only treatment for epilepsy was heavy sedation. Nobody dreamed an anticonvulsant drug factor could be developed that could stop convulsions without keeping the patient in a constant state of torpor or semisleep so that he can't function. Morgan is full of surprises. After this man left, he told us that it's necessary to differentiate between psychomotor epilepsy and catatonic excitement. Apparently catatonics sometimes (rarely, fortunately) go into an excited state almost identical with and just as destructive as epileptic equivalents. Of course, both are rare and in most cases of psychomotor attacks there may be no history at all of ordinary convulsive seizures. The history is usually helpful in making a differential diagnosis, as is the E.E.G., which is characteristically abnormal in epilepsy. Morgan then went on to tell us that he felt that both conditions are characterized by an inability to cope with anger. They both handle anger in an all-or-nothing way, either repressing it totally or expressing it uncontrollably and explosively. He says that the whole catatonic stiffness is probably an effort to hold back anger that the patient fears will destroy the world. He also says that epileptic people often have gigantic temper tantrums and angry outbursts that cannot be stopped, any more than their convulsions can, until they are completely spent. Nothing Morgan knows or says surprises me any more. Here he is a surgeon, full of all kinds of odd tidbits of neurological and psychiatric information. Maybe all of it is part of one field after all, the whole human structure.

We had another psychiatrically complicated case today. A woman came in, fifty years old, with a gash on her forehead. She was slightly drunk. As we sutured her, she kept repeating, "Look at me now, Ma—satisfied? Look at me now!" All the while she was saying this, she seemed quite happy with herself. I asked her about it, and all she would tell me was that it was her private little joke; and then she went on to say it again. What disease is that? Some kind of masochistic vindictive triumph directed against her mother? Could be.

I saw my first crush-syndrome case today. Morgan says

there were many of them in London during the bombings.
A building had caved in on this mason. His entire chest
and face were brick red, suffused with blood. But he had
no serious organ injuries. Apparently this is some kind of
vascular response to pressure on internal organs, maybe related to the kidneys in some way. Morgan says the red flush
will go away as capillaries close off. The guys looks in-
finitely worse off than he is.

Early this A.M. a woman, thirty-two, sort of nice looking,
came in with a bitten hand. We cleaned it up, gave her
T.A.T. and penicillin, and told her to report to the clinic
for follow-up. It was a human bite, possibly the most dangerous of all. When I asked her who did it, she said a John
under the boardwalk at Ocean Beach. I asked her to elaborate and she did. Simply stated, she said, "I'm a cock-
sucker"—just like that! When I looked puzzled or startled
or both, she matter-of-factly described how she made a
pretty good living under the boardwalk with Johns she
picked up on the boardwalk. She seemed to be of about
average intelligence and apparently had no sense of guilt
at all. I suppose she's an example of "psychopathy" or
"sociopathy." But is she any worse than a guy like Smithson? Lately he's in and out of here again, but he doesn't
go near Logan. I have a feeling something went on between them that I don't know about. Maybe she slugged
him or something. He's not really a bad guy. Aside from
his scoring obsession, he's rather serious and bright in general conversation. But he has no conscience whatsoever as
regards women. He feels anything is O.K.—any line, prom-

ise, or lie—in order to score. And of course he has this other "fault": like Morgan and Rog, he eats like a horse and doesn't put on a pound. Some day I'd like to have a weight-gaining problem. Imagine being told to try to eat hamburgers, spaghetti, malteds, etc., in order to try to put on weight. When I leave here I'll be 275 if I'm not careful.

I guess I've been avoiding it, the home-stretch feeling but it's true I'm almost done. I'm coming to the end of it: the E.R. interning and, I suppose, medicine as I always dreamed of it. Just a bit to go, and then I'm a freshman all over again, this time in psychiatry. Of course I'll miss it, the whole medical thing I've had in my head since I was a little kid. Until college psych it seemed impossible that anything could ever turn me off that road. Maybe it's that I'm beginning to feel a real sense of competency— and I'll miss that. No sooner do I become a kind of senior at something than I find I'm a freshman at something else all over again. The half-assed bitching and woes of the perpetual schoolboy.

Today we had a formal lecture on malpractice by a doctor who practices law (of course he's also a lawyer). The place was jammed. Guys must have taken off from busy practices in order to be there. This whole business of legal suits against M.D.s is really big stuff here in sunny California. All in all, it seems to make for some pretty difficult medicine. I suppose it keeps the would-be charlatans in some kind of check, but it also can be inhibiting and damaging as hell. To have to think of your legal ass before you say a word, make a decision, or initiate treatment can have a pretty lousy effect on what otherwise may have turned out to be sound medical judgment.

We had two victims of butane fires today, both children,

six and nine years old. No baby-sitter! It's another California habit, to leave kids alone at night. They were pretty bad. I guess I'm selfish—I'd really hoped not to see any more of these before I left. The medical enrichment of certain smells, sounds, and sights I can do without.

We also got a forty-eight-year-old woman tonight with intractable hiccoughs. She was terrified because the same thing had happened to her four years earlier, and it was so bad she couldn't eat or sleep for weeks. She said she lost so much weight (an angle for me) that people thought she had cancer. They tried everything and were about to do surgery to crush one of the branches of the phrenic nerve when she stopped. She says it had gone on for three and a half weeks. But this time was not that time, though I can hardly blame her for being traumatized by past history. She admitted that she had been hiccoughing now for only "an hour or so" and was very frightened (isn't fear supposed to stop hiccoughs?). I gave her some Luminal I.M. and O_2 by mask to make her feel that I took this very seriously—which I really did. I think the treatment of choice is CO_2, but this may be an old wives' tale. Anyway, she stopped and went home. My first and probably last case of intractable hiccoughs underwent, I suspect, a spontaneous cure—largely the result of reassurance.

Success with the hiccoughing lady must have gone to my head, because just a few hours ago, 1 A.M. to be almost exact, I did a real good piece of psychotherapy. We got a woman, fifty-two years old, in status asthmaticus. This was the worst case I've ever seen. This woman could get air out of her lungs hardly at all and was obviously in very serious respiratory distress. We gave her O_2, I.V., Benadryl, and adrenalin and aminophyllin with just about no visible evidence of relief at all. Finally we called in Johnson who told us over the phone that it might be necessary to get the anesthesiologist to give her general anesthesia to put her out. Apparently this sometimes breaks up this kind of attack and can be lifesaving. Anyway, he (Johnson) told us he'd be over as soon as possible.

While we waited I took her into a side room, sat next to her bed, and spoke to her as gently as I know how. Well, in no time at all she began to weep and then to cry louder and stronger, so that through her awful wheezing and gasping she was racked with sobbing. Then, as I listened, she began to talk and to cry—and as she talked and cried her choking and gasping began to disappear. I really feel as though I had in some way stepped into a medical miracle of some kind. She told me that she and her husband had been camping in the desert and that they had had a terrible fight. He took the car and went off. She's always been terrified of being alone. She was afraid that if she started to weep she would lose control and go into a complete panic. So she held herself in—she actually said, "I held myself all in"—and walked to the nearest house, which fortunately was only about a mile away. By the time she got there she couldn't breathe. As she finished getting the story and tears out, both Johnson and her husband arrived and she went home. Johnson told us that he feels that inheritance and psychosomatic factors both play a big role in bronchial asthma. He says that holding back tears and anger probably affects the adrenals and the diameter of the alveolar sacs, and that there's no question of the value of psychotherapy in "certain cases." Well, I don't know about Johnson, but I'm certainly impressed. I can see that listening and talking can be at least as powerful as O_2 and adrenalin and aminophyllin. I don't know how it works or if an analytic cure is possible, but when this woman started to ventilate emotionally she started to ventilate lung-wise too!

Speaking of miracles, we had a kid (twelve years old) and his aunt come off the coast highway this evening. They went into a ditch. She wasn't hurt, but he had multiple cuts and bruises and had lost considerable blood and was quite shocky. The aunt would not sign the necessary forms. They belong to some religious sect that does not permit the "transfer of blood." We told her that plasmoid is not blood. She said that she would not sign or take the responsibility, and that the kid's parents were off somewhere on a "pilgrimage" and couldn't be reached. We started the I.V. and called Madden, who said lawsuit be damned, go ahead anyway. We did, and of course I respect Madden, but I have to admit that with all this malpractice crap etc., I'm glad it's his ass and not mine. But I know in my gut I would have gone ahead anyway—I hope. Jesus, this state of California presents all kinds of combinations of special nonsense.

I took a nap today and dreamed that I was going up in an elevator (a Freudian heyday!) and then got scared and came down back to the ground and then somehow just moved sideways. Both Freud and Horney say associations are the clues to dreams. Going up sounds like getting an inflated picture of myself. Coming down could be coming down to earth, and going sideways brings zero. Maybe it means going off to psychiatry (psychiatry seen as sideways or adjacent to the rest of medicine), or maybe it means walking and being on solid ground, having realistic self-esteem rather than up-and-down stuff. This last interpretation sounds good, so I'll keep it. Why not? After all, it's *my* dream.

We got a guy today, forty-five years old, with absolutely no findings and no history to speak of. But he looked terrible. We went over him with a fine comb, and every system, temp, B.P., checked out normal. And yet the guy said he felt very weak and as though he was dying. I thought of the navy, where you had to have a certain temp to be put in sick bay or no dice, whatever your condition. Anyway, his doc, an internist I don't know, came in and looked him over and took him home. I thought he should have kept him here a few days. Is it possible to be dying without discernible findings? In any case, this was certainly a man that deserved hospital observation for a while, but this was one decision I had no butt-in rights on.

We got an addict today who was pretty obvious. The guy feigned symptoms of about twelve different syndromes. Nobody could be that sick and live. In the old days it didn't take much to throw me (old?—less than a year ago, and it seems like a lifetime). I feel torn by the addict thing. We all take a sort of glee in finding them out and throwing them out without treatment. To me this seems absolutely wrong. I hate to be manipulated by this guy or anyone else, but the guy is sick and I think we're remiss as doctors if we don't treat him in some way. Truth is I'm not even sure that the treatment of choice wouldn't be to make drugs available if he needs them so desperately. Legalize it all. Yet that stirs misgivings in me too. I just don't know. But kicking him out is lousy too!

Speaking of lousy, we got a battered child today. This little five-year-old girl was badly beaten up. Fortunately, we found no internal stuff and she went home to an aunt. The police told us her parents (twenty-three and twenty-one years old) are both in custody. We all felt we'd like to kill them. But aren't they sick too? I guess there are some sicknesses that we just can't abide. What are people like this? Psychopaths, I suppose. But I can't rise above it—thinking of that helpless kid even now makes me want to slowly strangle them.

Sailor is conscious! He's actually conscious and speaking! I wouldn't call it any big discussion, or even conversation. But we all ran up like crazy when his special called us, and he's awake, alive, and talking. He sounds confused and hazy, but he's talking in a low kind of mumble. He couldn't answer any questions, but he wiggled his fingers (despite his fractured shoulder) and opened and closed his eyes on command. He also wiggled his toes and let us know that he felt "pinpricks" all over. This guy has been unconscious for more than three months and he's going to come out of it. Jesus, I hope to God he doesn't slip back! Well, we went wild, absolutely wild. A bottle came out of somewhere (Smithson, I suspect), and we all had a bit of a celebration in a side room. Maybe we're crazy and cruel and uncaring, too: we've had more death and destruction down here in the last twenty-four hours than any other time since I've been on E.R., and none of us seems to care—because we now have concrete, real hope that Sailor will make it. Writing this reminds me of the girl who died in the accident with him. Wonder if he will remember her? There I go, being a killjoy. Truth is I haven't felt this good since I found out I passed my med school finals. Is this what the analysts mean by "emotional investment"?

Sailor will remain conscious, there's no question of that. He has bits and pieces of memory coming back, and more is getting clearer. He's becoming more responsive and seems to know who he is but not what's happened.

His parents came by today and looked so much better. His mother hugged and kissed each of us, and I had to go into a side room because I couldn't keep back the tears.

Peter Hennesy, the assistant pathologist, came in today and had Morgan excise a tiny mass on his leg he thought might be a neurofibroma. I went upstairs with him and looked at the slide, which was normal. I can't blame him for being nervous, working around this stuff all day. I admire these guys, the pathologists—it takes a special kind of fortitude to be constantly in the middle of death and malignancy.

Bad news comes with good: I got a letter today. My friend's multiple sclerosis is progressing very rapidly. He no longer has bladder control and can hardly walk. M.S. is known to remit for long periods of time for no reason that anyone understands. I hope this happens to him.

Sailor is very slowly getting pieces of himself back and together. The whole thing is just amazing. It's as if this guy is slowly developing and giving birth to himself all over again. Also, it's amazing how great his physical condition is. There's been some talk of transferring him to the naval hospital as soon as he's ready—he can get all kinds of rehabilitation therapy there. This kid is going to be O.K., and maybe this is true of the whole damned battered species of us when all is said and done.

But, of course, people continue to be self-destructive and crazy as hell.

I had a woman in here today, not drunk or anything else, who had walked through a glass door in her house that's been there twenty years. She doesn't know what got into her. Just forgot all about it.

A twenty-year-old girl used a sunlamp on herself to get tan—here in southern California—and forgot to wear sunglasses. We called in Jack Stamm, who says she will be O.K. but is very, very lucky.

A diabetic man, fifty-eight, with one leg already gone from the knee down, suddenly went blind in one eye while he was at the races. Maybe his B.P. shot up watching the horses. I thought of retinal detachment or hemorrhage. It was a central artery hemorrhage. Stamm said the eye is gone. The man said that he was a "good boy" except at the races, where he ate and drank what he wanted. Ice cream is his big thing, and he goes to the races at least three days a week. I'm sure the prohibition makes the thing all the more enticing. It's surely this way with me and my dieting. (I know it. So what?) He kept asking us over and over again if it was cancer, and we kept reassuring him that it wasn't. Then he kept repeating how grateful he is that it's not cancer. He didn't seem to give a damn about the blindness. Is this denial, a cancer phobia, or both? Or are they one and the same thing?

Sailor has been transferred to the naval hospital. They came and took him. The place seems funny without him. I guess we all feel glad and sad—and I feel like it's time for me to leave, too. Just a couple of days to go. Imagine Sailor gone! No one doubts he's going to be O.K. We lose some and win some, and he turned out to be a winner.

This afternoon I saw a guy with intractable headaches (maybe smog causes some of the bad headaches and throats around here?). Gave him Empirin and codeine and told him to report to the clinic. We were fully staffed and the place was empty, so I took off for a half hour—figured I'd take a walk. Well, the E.R. followed me out into the street.

I was walking along, only three blocks from the hospital, when I heard this hell of a noise like a crash. Then I saw what had happened: a car had veered off the road into a used-car lot and had smashed up about five of the used cars before it stopped. About twenty people—several cops and me included—ran over to see. All the time, I was thinking, here I am, out of the E.R. jurisdiction, still an intern even though with only a couple of days to go—and no Cal license to practice medicine yet. All the stuff about being sued by people you help on the street came back to me from the malpractice lecture. But I thought of Madden and the religious sect transfusion boy, and I pushed through to the car. The driver was an elderly man whose face was gray and rapidly turning black. The only thing I could think of doing was to give him mouth-to-mouth and a dry cardiac massage. But when I loosened his collar, I saw this 4 × 4 gauze pad and under it a permanent tracheotomy tube. This guy had probably had a C.A. of the larynx years ago and has been breathing through this tube ever since. Well, he wasn't breathing. I had a hunch that the tube gradually filled with mucus, cutting off his oxygen, and he passed out and veered off the road. I told one of the cops to quick get me a straw, which he did in seconds. I sucked out the guy's trache tube with it, pounded his chest a few times, and very dramatically (I must say so myself) he started to breathe normally, regained consciousness, and got normal color back in his face. By this time I thought of the legality of all of it again and got the hell out of there, telling the cop to bring him to the E.R. for a complete going-over. The guy didn't come, probably because he was O.K.

I saw a crazy one before I went off duty today. This woman, forty-one years old, came in with a nipple a quarter removed from the areola of her breast. She had normally sized breasts, actually on the small side—which is interesting because of the way she told us it happened. She said she got the breast caught in the window of her car. How this is possible I don't know. If someone tried it with her size breasts it would be impossible. But she did it—I believe her. Anyway, we taped it tight and Morgan said she'd be all right. He told us the classic nipple-off-breast story of the girl who is having her breast kissed by her boyfriend in the rumble seat of a car; the car goes over a bump and she loses the nipple when he bites down. I don't quite know why, but my association is the story of the guy who says he got V.D. in a bathroom and the doctor says, "That's a funny place to make love to your girl."

Kurt invited me to go home with him for dinner this evening, and I just couldn't turn him down. It wasn't for a future date, so there was no time to think about it. Also, it was to be just for an hour or so, and besides there's only another couple of days to go. Listen to all these rationalizations—what a lot of crap! I went because I've gotten to like the guy. Nazi and the whole business—and there it is! Anyway his wife and two kids (girls in their twenties) seemed really awfully nice—just warm, gracious people. They reminded me of Lausanne and the Swiss. On the way back he swore to me that he joined because of fear and just because he was a conformist and weak and would not be able to make a living otherwise. He said he had no idea what it was all about and never had a political feeling one way or the other in his life. He said he was never a Nazi in feelings or action. Thank God he didn't make with the Jewish-best-friend or liking-Jews bit. Who knows? It's easy as hell to be hateful and judgmental, and almost as easy to be forgiving. But it's a lot harder to feel it all at the same time, and that's how I feel—confused as hell. My grandfather was killed by anti-Semites in a pogrom in Russia. Maybe someday I'll understand it but I can't forget it—or forgive it—not yet, anyway.

I understand the trache man I sucked out on the street came around to the hospital to thank me, but we missed each other.

Logan, the cold one, gave me a beautiful cashmere sweater that she'd knitted as a going-away present. The other girls had chipped in for the wool. Then each of them kissed me—the Log, too—warmly and gently. I couldn't keep from crying, and Logan actually cried, too.

Quistle called me in and told me that he'd heard all about the trache man on the street, from a cop and the man himself. I thought, here it is, my last day and I'm about to be hit by a lawsuit or something. But instead he said that the hospital was very proud of me and all that stuff, and would I consent to a big publicity spread on it? They thought they could get it into a national magazine and on T.V. I said *no!* Just like that—no! Maybe the $1,000 is still burning me up, or maybe it's false modesty, or maybe it's that I feel it's inappropriate to fuss about something no one would think twice about if it had happened in the E.R. But whatever it was, I felt in my guts that for me no was a good answer, and it felt good to say it. He then congratulated me on being an excellent intern and said he was sure I'd be a very good psychologist. The s.o.b. doesn't even know the difference between a psychologist and a psychiatrist!

———

I got a call from Madden today here at the V.A. They need extra help, and he thought of me. Any Sat.or Sun. that I'm off at the V.A., I can do ten hours a day at $15. Of course I said yes. I guess I'm flattered—and I miss the place and can use the $30 extra a week. Out of the clear blue—I didn't ask him—Madden tells me he finally had to amputate Carpenter's leg. But he said he heard that Sailor is doing great. My internship must really be over—because through all this he actually called me Ted!

EMERGENCY ROOM MEDICAL TERMS AND HOSPITAL JARGON

Ace. Elasticized bandage.

Acute catatonia. A psychotic state in which the individual becomes physically rigid and psychologically cut off from the world around him.

Adenitis. Inflammation of a lymph gland.

Adrenalin. A substance secreted by the adrenal glands that makes capillaries contract and heart beat faster.

Anaerobic gas bacilli. Very destructive bacilli that produce deadly gas in an atmosphere lacking oxygen, such as within deep wounds.

Anaphylaxis. A severe allergic reaction that can cause death by edema of lungs due to the increased permeability of blood vessels that allows abnormal amounts of fluid to go into tissue spaces from bloodstream.

Anastomosis. A process in which two ends are put together, as when a section of intestine is removed and the two remaining ends are joined. Also refers to the extra blood vessels present in older age.

Aneurysm. A sac formed by the bulging out of part of an artery.

Anticoagulant. A substance used to slow up the coagulation of the blood; often used in coronary thrombosis.

A.P. Appendicitis or appendectomy.

Areola. The pink area immediately around the nipple of the breast.

Arrhenoblastoma. A malignant tumor of the ovary, reputedly the most malignant cancer of all.

Attending. Short for attending staff, physicians who practice privately and who use the hospital for their patients when necessary. For this privilege they have teaching and other hospital responsibilities.

Axilla. Armpit.

Balloon test. A test used to determine the alcohol content of blood.

Basal cell epithelioma. A cancerous growth on the skin that can be destructive in its immediate vicinity, but which neither spreads nor kills.

Benadryl. One of the antihistamine drugs.

Bifurcation of common iliac. The arterial fork, located in the pelvis, where the common iliac artery branches to go down both lower limbs.

Blowout of the duodenal stump. A complication following gastrectomy in which remaining end of duodenum opens up.

Bougie. A dilating instrument.

B.P. Blood pressure.

Bronchial asthma. A chest condition involving difficult breathing, in which wheeze is produced in the labored effort to expel breath.

C.A. Cancer.

Caffeine sodium benzoate. A drug used as a heart stimulant.

Capillaries. The smallest blood vessels in the body.

Carbuncle. A boil.

Caruncle. An infected hair follicle.

Cellulitis. Inflammation of the skin, often with arterial involvement causing a streak on the skin superficial to an artery. The causative organism is usally streptococcus and can cause septicemia (blood poisoning) if neglected.

Cerebral. Referring to the brain.

Cheyne-Stokes respiration. Rhythmic alteration of the intensity of breathing, often characteristic of impending death in strokes and heart attacks.

Cholecystectomy. Surgical removal of the gall bladder.

Colles's fracture. Simple wrist fracture of the distal ends of radius and ulna.

Colostomy. A surgical procedure, sometimes used in treatment of cancer of the rectum, in which the large intestine is brought out through a hole in the abdomen.

Compound fracture. Fracture in which bone fragments penetrate the skin and are exposed.

Coramine. A drug used as a heart stimulant.

Cornea. The transparent anterior part of the eye.

Coronaries. The arteries feeding the heart muscle intrinsically.

Coronary. Short for coronary occlusion, usually due to coronary thrombosis; common form of "heart attack."

Crenated erythrocyte. A dried-up shrunken red blood cell.

Cubital fossa. The anatomical area directly in front of the elbow.

Cut-down. A procedure necessary when a vein cannot be found to provide for an intravenous transfusion. An incision is made over the expected site of a vein in order to expose and use the vein for transfusion.

C.V.A. Cerebro-vascular accident, commonly known as a stroke, usually caused by either a cerebral hemorrhage, cerebral thrombus, or cerebral embolus.

Cyanosis. Blue-tinged lips due to lack of proper oxygenation; a common clinical sign in heart attacks.

Debride. To cut away dead tissue.

Dex. Dexedrine or amphetamine stimulant.

Diabetes. A chronic disease involving faulty sugar metabolism.

Diathane. Anesthetic rectal ointment.

Differential diagnosis. The listing of the various possible diagnostic entities that may exist in a given condition.

Digitalis. A specific drug used to strengthen heart contractions.

Diuretic. Any kidney stimulant.

D.O.A. Dead on arrival.

Dry phlebotomy. A procedure in which tourniquets are applied to the limbs to relieve heart of total body blood. It achieves the same effect as a phlebotomy, which is the surgical opening up of a vein to permit bleeding.

Dyspnea. Labored or difficult breathing.

Ecchymosis. Extravasation of blood into tissue spaces.

E.C.T. Electro-convulsive or electro-shock therapy.

Edema. Swelling.

Electrolyte. Any substance that in solution conducts electric currents.

Elephantiasis. Chronic lymphangitis, disturbing lymph circulation and resulting in hypertrophy of the skin.

Embolus. A moving clot or plug that can obstruct a blood vessel.

Endocarditis. Inflammation of the endocardium (the inner lining of the heart), sometimes a complication of rheumatic fever.

Enucleate. To take out whole; specifically, the surgical removal of an eye.

E.N.T. Ear, nose, and throat.

E.R. Emergency room.

Erythrocyte. Red blood cells.

Esophageal. Referring to the esophagus, the section of the digestive tract located between the pharynx and the stomach.

Extrasystoles. Extra (out of regular rhythm) heart contractions.

Films. X-ray photographs.

Foley. Short for a Foley catheter, an indwelling urinary catheter left in place for a prolonged period and used in comatose and post-operative patients who do not have sufficient bladder control.

Fracture reduction. Putting fractured bone fragments in proper position.

Furacin. An antiseptic, soothing substance that comes in liquid and Vaseline-consistency form.

Ganglion. Any mass of gray nervous substance that serves as a center of nervous influence.

Gastrectomy. Surgical removal of the stomach.

General anesthesia. A state of deep sleep, usually induced by drugs, during which pain is not felt.

General paresis. A general paralysis; the end stage of syphilis, which is characterized by paralysis and psychosis.

Globus hystericus. A subjective sensation of fullness in throat.

Grand mal. A convulsive seizure, as in epilepsy.

Gusher. A cut artery.

Hebephrenia. A form of schizophrenia marked by child-like, silly, disorganized behavior.

Hematoma. A bump of blood under the skin.

Hirschsprung's disease. A congenital much enlarged colon (large intestine); congenital mega-colon.

Histamine. A bodily substance released into the blood during allergic responses that makes capillaries more permeable.

Humerus. The bone between the shoulder and elbow.

Hyperventilation. Abnormally deep and fast breathing.

Hypnotic. Any drug that induces sleep.

Hypochondriasis. The state of being a hypochondriac; having an exaggerated fear of sickness.

I.M. Intramuscular.

Infarct. A wedge-shaped area of the heart muscle that has been deprived of blood (due to coronary occlusion) and thus dies. This is a common form of "heart attack."

Intracardiac. Within the heart; an intracardiac injection is an injection into the heart itself.

Intracranial. Within the skull.

Intracutaneous. Within the skin; as distinct from subcutaneous, under the skin.

Iris. The colored part of the eye.

I.V. Intravenous.

I.V.P. Intravenous pylogram, a special X-ray study of the urinary tract, for which special dye is injected into the vein.

Lacunae. Holes; vacuums; empty spaces.

Laryngeal edema. Swelling of the larynx, which can cause asphyxiation and death; sometimes present in severe allergy.

Levine tube. A simple long rubber tube used to insert in stomach, either through mouth or nose.

Luminal. A specific hypnotic drug.

Lymphangitis. Inflammation of lymph tissues.

Maxilla. The upper jawbone.

Melanoma. A very malignant skin cancer arising from a pigmented nevus.

Meningitis. Inflammation of the meninges (pia mater, dura mater, arachnoid), the brain and spinal cord tissue coverings.

Metal corneal implant. A metal splinter embedded in the cornea.

Metastasis. The spreading of cancer from the primary site to secondary sites.

Mitril thrill. The vibration caused by closure of the mitril valve of the heart.

Moribund. In a dying state.

Multiple myeloma. A type of cancer involving lymph glands all over the body.

Na (sodium) Amital. A drug used for sedation and sleep. It has property of making people reveal the unconscious; sometimes used in catatonic states.

NaCl. Sodium chloride (table salt).

Nasal O_2 catheter. A tube in the nose, through which oxygen is administered.

Neoplasm. Literally, "new growth"; refers to tumors, benign and malignant.

Neuroma. A growth made up largely of nerve substance.

Nevus. A skin mole.

O_2. Oxygen.

Occipital. Referring to the back of the skull.

Omentum. A reduplication (or fold) of the peritoneum, going from the stomach to the adjacent organs.

Osteo. Short for osteomyelitis.

Osteomyelitis. Inflammation of the bone.

Otitis media. Inflammation of the middle ear.

Paralytic ileus. A condition in which peristalsis—the successive waves of contraction of the small intestine that move the contents along—has stopped.

Patella. The superficial movable knee bone—the kneecap.

Pathognomonic. Distinctively characteristic of a particular disease process.

Peritonitis. Inflammation of the peritoneum, the tissue covering the abdominal organs.

Phenobarbital. A sedative and hypnotic drug.

Phrenic nerve. The nerve stimulating and controlling diaphragmatic muscle.

Pigmented nevus. A dark mole.

Placebo. A medicine or pseudo-medicine given as suggestive treatment to soothe a patient.

Plasmoid. Plasma (the liquid part of the blood) in a dry preparation, mixed with water.

Pneumonitis. Inflammation of the lung.

Post-mortem. An autopsy.

Pott's fracture. Fracture of ankle, involving the lower tibia and the fibula.

Prefrontal lobectomy. Surgical removal of a small amount of tissue from the frontal lobes of the brain.

Prefrontal lobotomy. An incision into brain tissue to sever nerve connections in the frontal lobes. (This procedure, like the *prefrontal lobectomy,* is a controversial treatment modality sometimes used in cases of chronic severe psychosis.)

Prn. As needed.

Psychomotor equivalent. A form of epilepsy in which wild behavior, including violent body action, supplants convulsions.

Psychomotor retardation. The slowdown of all bodily movement in severe emotional depression.

Psychopath or sociopath. A person with a paucity of conscience and a tendency to antisocial behavior.

Pulmonary bifurcation. The arterial fork, located in the chest, where the pulmonary artery branches to go to each lung.

Rales. Any abnormal respiratory sound heard in auscultation (examination through a stethoscope).

Radical mastectomy. Surgical removal of the breast and all of the lymph glands around it and in the area of the sternum (breast bone) and armpit.

Rebound tenderness. A painful response when the abdominal wall is allowed to rebound after being pushed in; characteristic of appendicitis.

Refer. To send a patient to another doctor.

Remit or Remission. A quiescent stage, or the disappearance, of a disease.

Renal colic. Kidney pain, usually very severe, caused by kidney stones.

Rotating internship. A period of medical training in which a prescribed amount of time is spent on each of the various services of the hospital (internal medicine, obstetrics, surgery, etc.) as an intern.

Schizophrenia. A poorly understood psychotic condition characterized by hallucinations, delusions, and inappropriate affect.

Sensorium. Any sensory nerve center.

Service cases. Non-paying hospital ward patients.

Shock. A state in which blood pressure drops markedly and death ensues unless intervention takes place.

Simple fracture. A fracture in which the cracked bones do not penetrate the skin.

Simple mastectomy. Removal of the breast alone, and not the surrounding lymph glands.

Skin test. A test in which a scratch or small injection containing possible allergic substance is made. If allergy is present there is a red swelling response.

Special. A private nurse.

Spleen capsule. The thin tough membrane around the spleen.

Splenectomy. Surgical removal of the spleen, a non-vital organ.

Stat! Immediately! At once!

Status asthmaticus. A severe and prolonged asthmatic attack.

Subdural. Under the dura, one of the meninges or brain coverings.

Sympathizing eye. An otherwise healthy eye that is affected when the *other* eye has been badly traumatized. Unless the damaged eye is removed, blindness will ensue in the sympathizing eye. No one can predict if this sympathetic reaction will or will not take place. The mechanism that produces this phenomenon is unknown.

Systemic. Throughout the whole body.

T.A.T. Tetanus antitoxin.

Thrombus. A clot in a blood vessel, adherent to the vessel wall and thus stationary.

Treponema pallidum. The bacillus that causes syphilis.

Type and cross-match. To determine blood type and check against donor blood for transfusion.

Upstairs. The rest of the hospital, other than the E.R.

Venopuncture. A hole in a vein, such as is made for an intravenous injection.

Welch bacillus. Gas-forming bacillus.

Whiplash fracture. Fracture of the neck caused by a jolt forward in auto trauma.

White count. White-blood-cell count, which becomes increased in infections and other conditions.

H.S.

ABOUT THE AUTHOR

Theodore Isaac Rubin is married, has three children, and lives and works in New York City.

He is a graduate of Brooklyn College, where he majored in psychology, and received his M.D. degree from the Faculty of Medicine of the University of Lausanne, Switzerland.

He did a rotating internship in a medium-size, non-profit community general hospital in southern California. The emergency room department of that hospital was one of the most active in the state. Dr. Rubin spent one-third of his internship on the emergency room service.

He did his first year of psychiatric residency at the V.A. Hospital in Los Angeles and during that time continued to work in the E.R. of his internship hospital on off-duty weekends. Dr. Rubin completed his psychiatric training at Rockland State Hospital, Brooklyn State Hospital, and Kings County Hospital. He subsequently trained and was certified by the American Institute for Psychoanalysis. He is currently the president of the Institute and a training and supervising psychoanalyst. He is also on the board of the Karen Horney Clinic and a fellow of the American Academy of Psychoanalysis.